S0-BSH-944

10/24
STRAND PRICE
5.00

BY *AGNES REPPLIER*

675

(*IN PURSUIT OF*

LAUGHTER)

*Un gros rire vaut mieux
qu'une petite larme.*

PROPERTY OF
BOARD OF EDUCATION
NOV 29 1944
CITY OF NEW YORK

EASTERN DISTRICT HIGH SCHOOL
827 Marcy Avenue—Brooklyn, N. Y.

Boston and New York
HOUGHTON MIFFLIN COMPANY
The Riverside Press Cambridge

COPYRIGHT, 1936, BY AGNES REPPLIER

ALL RIGHTS RESERVED INCLUDING THE RIGHT TO REPRODUCE
THIS BOOK OR PARTS THEREOF IN ANY FORM

The Riverside Press
CAMBRIDGE · MASSACHUSETTS
PRINTED IN THE U.S.A.

CONTENTS

824
R

8897

IN PURSUIT OF LAUGHTER

I

BEFORE LAUGHTER WAS PURSUED

How high the sea of human delight rose in the Middle Ages, we know only by the colossal walls they built to keep it within bounds. But now there is a certain grief in things as they are, in man as he has come to be.

CHESTERTON

I

BEFORE LAUGHTER WAS PURSUED

EASTERN DISTRICT HIGH SCHOOL
227 Marcy Avenue—Brooklyn, N. Y.

No MAN pursues what he has at hand. No man recognizes the need of pursuit until that which he desires has escaped him. Those who listen to the Middle Ages instead of writing about them at monstrous length and with undue horror and commiseration, can hear the echo of laughter ringing from every side, from every hole and corner where human life existed. Through the welter of wars and famine and pestilence, through every conceivable disaster, through an atmosphere darkened with ignorance and cruelty and needless pain there emerges, clear and unmistakable, that will to live which man shares with the beast, and which means that, consciously or unconsciously, he finds life worth the living. Henry James, in whom the disease of thinking had reached an acute stage, expressed his wistful envy of 'the stoutness of the human composition in medieval days, and the tranquillity of nerve of people to whom the groaning captive and the blackness of the living tomb were familiar ideas, which did not at all interfere with their happiness or their sanity.'

They probably interfered somewhat with the happiness of those immediately concerned — with the wife and children of the prisoner. But in the soothing absence of newscarriers, there was no general commotion. Even in these days of wires and wireless, when nobody has a chance to be ignorant, we do not make ourselves unhappy over the yearly hecatomb that follows the wake of the motor, or over the fact that our convicts emerge unbidden from their 'living tomb' to pillage and slay their fellow creatures. That 'work of mercy' enjoined upon early Christians, 'to visit and ransom the captive,' did not mean letting loose the thug and the gangster to prey upon a seemingly defenceless world.

It is strange that so little attention should have been paid to the gaiety of the Middle Ages, which is as characteristic as the passionate devotion of their saints, or as the callous cruelty of their sinners. It is strange that the sound of laughter should not more often silence the sound of weeping, or muffle the murmur of prayer. Now and then this unfamiliar aspect strikes an observant reader so powerfully that, in its turn, it interferes with the general perspective. Elizabeth Robins Pennell, contemplating convent and castle and town, reached the conclusion that when the Western world was young it was on the whole a very merry world. 'Drollery,' she wrote in one of her earlier essays, 'was the order of the day. Artisans and nobles, peasants and serfs, high and low, all dearly loved a jest, and all went chaffing through life as if it were a carnival, and one's only aim was to amuse and be amused. There was a grotesqueness and charm about the mischief of those days which had never been before, and which can never be again.'

Mrs. Pennell admits that medieval humour was mainly mischievous. 'Mischief characterizes the childhood and youth of the human race.' Somebody was expected to be the sufferer by a joke, and public sympathy supported the joker. Laughter springs from the lawless part of our nature, and is purifying only in so far as there is a natural unschooled goodness in the human heart. The question asked by Panurge, 'Can any man be as wise as are the devils?' and answered by Pantagruel, 'Nay, save by God's especial grace,' was a familiar query in the Middle Ages. Their God was not the irritable Deity of John Knox; and their Satan instead of 'fiercely stirring his terrible tail,' as Knox wrote to the brethren in Scotland, condescended to play fantastic pranks in law-courts and monasteries. He was an astute bargainer for the souls of men, yet was often outwitted and cheated 'by God's especial grace.' As Friar Rush, he toiled in the kitchen, concocting rare dishes out of unsavoury scraps, and intoxicating cordials out of thin wine. The bewildered friars, gluttonous and drunken, were easily led into sin; and only the wisdom and piety of a learned abbot, who pitted the power of the Church against the powers of darkness, saved them from damnation. The incomparable cook was turned into an ass, and driven ignominiously from the gates. The kitchen was purified and blessed, order and discipline were restored, and the friars ate plain fare, which must have seemed to them plainer than ever, for the rest of their chastened lives.

Sin was as great an imprudence to medieval Christians as it was to the ancient Jews, and Hell was as close to them, and as sure a thing, as it was to the Calvinists of Geneva. But there were more avenues of escape than Moses or Calvin were prepared to grant. Every certain sinner was a possible saint, and the frequency of the transformation throws an engaging light over the annals of imperfect humanity.

Courtesans atoned for their misdeeds in penitential solitude; and splendid young noblemen disappeared from the world which they had adorned and polluted to end their days in a particularly comfortless monastery. The colossal walls built by the Church to keep the sea of human delight within bounds held close at hand and always under consideration 'the four things to be remembered' — death, judgment, Heaven and Hell. But death was a familiar happening, easy to come by, and merciful in proportion to the swiftness of its approach. It was no great boon to die in one's bed with the medieval leech in attendance. Nothing can better illustrate the mental attitude which so amazed Henry James than the story of William of the Crooked Nose, a famed, but not always fortunate, fighter of the eleventh century. Long absent at war, he returned, spent, wounded and alone, to his Norman keep. His lady, Guibourc, opened the gates, and asked after his squires — Vivian, Bertram, and young Bernard. Where were they? Dead, all of them, and other good men as well. Stunned, she listened to his tale, and, when it was told, said simply, 'Wash your hands, lord, and come and eat.'

Manifestly the best thing to do. There were brighter days in store for William of the Crooked Nose, and less disastrous battle-fields. But the dead were dead. It was left for the living to dine.

'And after death comes judgment.' This, too, was inevitable, and monks and nuns had plenty of time to prepare for it. But for men who died in the heat of battle the good God would make allowances. The prayer of the old Cavalier: 'Lord, if I forget Thee this day, do not Thou forget me!' has always been the soldier's supplication. Pious sinners of the Middle Ages based their hope of Heaven on the kindly intercession of the saints who knew what life was like. As for Hell, it may be that if the Church had not held its peculiar terrors so persistently before their eyes, they would have feared it more. It is not well to be too precise when precision rests on the evidence of things unseen. Augustus Jessopp tells us of a Lincolnshire farmer who, having listened to a realistic sermon on Hell-fire, summed up his doubts briefly to the wife of his bosom: 'Noä, Sally, it woänt do. Noä constitootion could stan' it.'

The medieval attitude was one of simple acceptance, unaccompanied by that desolation of fear which drove brooding minds to madness. 'Hell-mouth' was a popular feature of many miracle plays. A horrid gaping cavern belching out flames, with imps darting about, herding the souls of the damned into their appointed place. It was terrifying, but it was also comical, because stage demons are inevitably comic, and the untutored crowd that watched their antics was always ready to laugh. A certain intimacy came to be established between man and his arch-enemy who lost a great deal by making himself so cheap. Monkish scholars remembered that the great Origen had always held the repentance of Satan and his final pardon to be a possibility. A story handed down from the terrible days of Attila said that, when the 'scourge of God' lay dying, a rumour spread throughout Hell that he would be sent to rule over it; and the poor damned souls ventured to offer a petition to the Most High, entreating that they might be left to the comparative kindness of their rightful master. Guibert de Nogent admitted that his fervour in prayer excessively irritated the Devil — a not uncommon point of view for the

7

twelfth century, and one which Martin Luther adopted later
for his own. There was a sense of intimacy about it fatal to
fearfulness.

Such being the case, it was the part of the Church to ter-
rify rather than to soothe, to sadden rather than to cheer.
Happiness was centred in the hope of Heaven, and earth
was a place of exile; not — as men persisted in thinking — a
place of enjoyment. The great hymns were, with the exception of the *Te Deum*, hymns of warning and of sorrow. The
Dies Irae and the *Stabat Mater* — both of the thirteenth century — bade sinners tremble for their souls, and good Christians weep for the holy Mother's pain. The *Salve Regina*,
most celebrated of the four Breviary anthems of the Blessed
Virgin, is an epitome of medieval invocation. It was written in the twelfth century, and was first chanted by the
monks of Cluny in 1135. It was destined to arouse the ire
of Luther who anathematized it with severity. It is a litur-
gical prayer, familiar to all Roman Catholics today; and
it is the passionate supplication of the unhappy. 'To thee
do we cry, poor banished children of Eve, to thee do we
send up our sighs, mourning and weeping in this valley of
tears.' It is probable that the monks of Cluny were not
mourning and weeping as they moved in solemn procession
in 1135; and to the congregations who in 1936 dutifully
repeat the prayer, these words have no literal significance.
But the *Salve Regina* represents exactly the mental attitude
which the medieval Church commended. It was a stone
in the wall which kept the sea of human delight within
bounds. We can always tell what generations of men were
like by the efforts of their mentors to make them otherwise.

8

Of what avail were these penitential exercises in silencing the laughter of the world? No one is disposed to doubt the religious fervour of the Middle Ages. Indeed the reproach most frequently cast at them is that their behaviour did not keep pace with their piety, human nature being as notoriously imperfect then as now. But pious as they were, they carried their jests straight into the fabric of the Church, into its ritual as well as into its architecture. The Boy Bishop who held sway from the feast of Saint Nicholas to the feast of the Holy Innocents, a matter of three weeks, must have been a serious nuisance to sober clerical authority. True, he owed his dignity to the kind patron of children. True, the clerics — making a virtue of necessity — helped to appoint him. True, he and his train of clerks were acolytes or choristers, well versed in ceremonial, and with some store of Latin. Edward the First, en route to his Scottish victories in 1298, heard them sing vespers at Newcastle-upon-Tyne, and made the Bishop a handsome gift of money. Nevertheless a boy is perilously full of original sin, and three weeks is a long time to keep a usurper within bounds. Priests and prelates must have heaved a sigh of relief when the Feast of the Holy Innocents restored the old order.

As for the Feast of Fools, it sounds to us today like an unmitigated horror of profanity. So, indeed, it appeared to Odo, Archbishop of Sens in 1265. So it did to Eudes de Sully, Archbishop of Paris in 1199. So it did to Robert Grosseteste, Bishop of Lincoln, and to other ecclesiastics who strove for years to modify what they could not suppress. The common people loved every familiar joke. They were not easily shocked. Their deeply rooted faith was untouched. They resisted obstinately every attempt to deprive them of

9

the recurrent tomfoolery at which they had laughed as children, and at which their fathers and their fathers' fathers had laughed before them. It took the authority of the Council of Basle, with the strong support of the University of Paris, to put a final end in 1435 to this relic of heathendom which had survived so many centuries of Christianity.

There is a tendency in these earnest days to explain seriously and a trifle sadly the 'bestiaries' carved on pillar and portal and choir stalls of medieval cathedrals. Grinning apes, sly foxes, and those unclassified animals that occasionally devour their arch-enemy, man, indicate, we are told, the dynamic force of evil, and prove the lurking presence of the great Manichean heresy. Imps and demons are not excluded. The Devil broods over the vastness of Notre Dame, and shares with Saint Genevieve a perpetual watch over Paris. He has his place in the hierarchy of creation. That medieval architects and sculptors and stonecutters and wood-carvers should have made a jest of the droll and unblessed creatures that display themselves with such effrontery seems too simple an explanation of their presence. Yet a fox chasing a fleeing huntsman was certainly humorous; and a cat eating a mouse under the bed of a sleeping monk had the homely charm of familiarity. Henry Adams, who wrote about the Middle Ages as though he had lived in them, had the courage to say that the swarming animals of Chartres were designed to amuse the Holy Virgin, in whose honour the cathedral was built. Certainly the queen who stands in the north portal with her feet resting on a monkey, two dragons, a dog and a basilisk might have won a smile from Heaven.

For Chartres was peculiarly and exceptionally a gift to the Mother of God. It was made flawless and superb so that she might delight in its beauty. It was made vast because, being liable to have ten thousand petitioners, she needed space for their accommodation. Soldiers were her most vociferous clients, and cried her name upon the battle-field; but all men were free to call themselves Our Lady's Servitors, or Our Lady's Sinners, according to their claims. She was the triumphant Virgin of the *Magnificat.* She was the Queen of Heaven, and a powerful pleader at the heavenly court. Above all she was mortal, a part of humanity, and as such more concerned with mercy than with justice. Henry Adams illustrates this important point with some startling stories, and with quotations from a long poem by Gaultier de Coincy, prior and poet of the early thirteenth century. In its pages the devils protest against the unfairness of the Blessed Virgin's influence at the tribunal of Heaven. What, they ask not unreasonably, is Hell made for save to accommodate sinners? Yet when all is ready for their reception, she interferes and snatches them from its dark gates:

> God judges us so true
> That He leaves us all our due.
> His Mother judges us so short
> That she throws us out of court
> When we ought to win our cause.

It is plain that even the prior considers the lenient patronage of the Virgin to be a trifle subversive of law.

Yet how gracious she was, how sweet, how understanding! She stepped down from her niche in the monastery chapel to fan with 'a fair white towel' the acrobat who lay exhausted at her feet. For the 'Tombeor de Notre Dame' was not a *jongleur*, but a humble *sauteur*, who could honour the holy Mother of God only by leaping and tumbling before her image. With ready kindness she darned the haircloth shirt of Saint Thomas à Becket, knowing the awkwardness of men with their needles. She was like a great feudal lady protecting her own, and far too sure of her high estate to fear a loss of dignity.

Such a lady would naturally expect to hold some intercourse with her retainers. Of all the charming tales told about the saints of God, no one is so charming as that of Saint Thomas Aquinas hurrying as fast as so heavy a man could hurry along the corridor of the monastery to vespers. As he passed a statue of the Blessed Virgin, it opened its lips and said admonishingly, 'Thomas, you are late.' To which the saint replied, also admonishingly, 'Mary, it is the hour of silence.'

What a story! What a perfect story! Men took it for granted that the Mother of God was as intelligent as she was flawless; but they gave little thought to her mentality. For twelve hundred years she had listened to her own praises, and to the supplications of her children who stood in need of help. That was her *métier*, and it held in it the element of monotony. Then Aquinas, the master mind of the thirteenth century, and one of 'the great liberators of the human intelligence,' met her fairly and squarely with the retort courteous. We can hear her laugh of delight echoed gaily by attendant angels; and it was the element of laughter that seemed so natural to great and humble, rich and poor, in the intimacy of the Middle Ages. They have been called 'hard, 'penitential, warlike, and migratory,' and they were all these things. But their sons were in love with life:

> Light-heart and gay
> Goes many a beggar by the way,

says the poet who wrote the 'Romance of the Rose.' He was of course unacquainted with statistics of medieval beggary, which would have been very distressing had there been any. But he had every opportunity to observe, and this cheerful summary was the result of his observation.

It was not the beggar only who went 'light-heart and gay' along the English highroads. They swarmed with tinkers, peddlers, 'toth-drawers,' needle-sellers (a special trade), acrobats, and artisans, all of whom, according to Langland, spent their earnings or their thievings in taverns, drinking and laughing until 'eve-song rang,' which was at eight o'clock. The author of 'Piers Plowman' had little sympathy with these vagabonds; but every village — tired of its own company — welcomed the wanderer who brought news from the next village, or possibly from the nearest town. The medieval fairs, like the Goose Fair at Nottingham and Saint Giles Fair at Winchester, drew hordes of these itinerants, who added nothing to the well-being of the farmers, and nothing to the tithes of the overlords, but a great deal to the merriment of the crowd. Jusserand says that the most cheerful cheats were the herbalists, whose remedies were infallible, and whose profits, if small, were sure. Rutebeuf's thirteenth-century herbalist, whom Jusserand quotes with delight, is of course a fraud; but he is persuasive, obliging and reasonable. He sells his life-giving herb for a penny, though it is worth many times that price, 'because a man may have a penny in his purse though he hath not a pound.' The leaves should be steeped in white wine if the purchaser has white wine; if not, he may use red. If he has no wine, he may take instead fine clear water, 'because many a man hath a well before his door who hath not a cask of wine in his cellar.'

Compare this accommodating, this magnanimous spirit with the rigid attitude of modern practitioners who make no allowance for an empty cellar or an empty purse.

Better men than herbalists and toth-drawers followed the open road. There were wandering minstrels and glee-men, and there were pilgrims galore, for the crusaders had awakened interest in holy places, and an aftermath of pilgrimages was the result. Langland disapproved of pilgrims as heartily as he disapproved of minstrels, whose rewards he considered excessive; but both were popular with the public, and pilgrims were largely in men's minds when bridge-building ranked as a meritorious deed. Saint Michael, patron of travellers, escorted the souls of bridge-builders to Heaven, and saw to it that they were well received. Medieval bridges were as strong as medieval churches, as beautiful in their way, and sometimes as devout. There still stands on the bridge at Wakefield the lady chapel built in the fourteenth century. 'A faire bridge of stone of nine arches, under which runneth the river of Calder, and on the east side of this bridge is a right goodly chapel of Our Lady, and two cantuarie preestes founded in it.' Hugh of Clopton's bridge, 'a great and sumptuous bridge,' still stands at Stratford-on-Avon, and shows to the world what a good citizen and a lord mayor of London stood ready to do at his own cost for the public weal before the fifteenth century drew to a close.

14

One of the reproaches cast upon pilgrims by Langland and William Thorpe and many another critic was their cheerfulness of demeanour. They travelled for the most part in groups for safety's sake, and they passed the time as merrily as they could. Chaucer did not object to this merriment, being himself a mirth-loving man. He laughs a little at his Canterbury pilgrims — at most of them — but not unkindly. He has no greater fancy for his Friar and Summoner than they have for each other. He says a caustic word in the Envoy to the Clerk's Tale concerning the rarity of patient and sweet-tempered women. But there is no animosity in his heart, and no love of sermonizing in his blood. His characters travel in seemly fashion. Their way is short. They are comfortable as well as entertaining. But when we turn from romance to reality we hear Thomas Arundel, Archbishop of Canterbury, expressing a kindly and sensible opinion. The poorer pilgrim who limped on bleeding feet did well, he thought, to be cheerful, to sing and laugh and jest; 'for with soche solace the travell and weariness of pylgrimage is lightely and merily broughte forthe.'

How poor many of these wayfarers were is evidenced by the help they received. The Guild of the Resurrection, founded in Lincoln in 1374, had this kindly rule: 'If any brother or sister wishes to make a pilgrimage to Rome, to Saint James of Galicia, or to the Holy Land, he shall forewarn the guild; and all the bretheren and the sisteren shall goe with him to the city gate, and each shall give him a halfpenny at least.' The tailors of Lincoln, not to be outdone, gave, each of them, to any tailor who went to Rome a halfpenny, and a penny if he went to the Holy Land.

The discomforts of the road were light when compared to

the discomforts of the sea, and the fatigue of the road was pleasurable when compared to the suffering and weariness entailed by a sea voyage. The dull and monotonous days were unbroken by any form of amusement. Reading for entertainment belonged to the far-away future. Even draughts were unknown. To soldiers such journeys were more insupportable than to pilgrims, for pilgrims could recite prayers and chant hymns, and soldiers could only quarrel and bet. Froissart tells us the story of a thirteenth-century knight who, sailing for the Scottish coast, was so oppressed by the lack of incident that he wagered he could climb the mast, clad in his heavy armour. His companions strove, as in duty bound, to dissuade him; but were prob-ably keen to see the feat attempted. Up went the knight until he was more than half way to the top; then his foot slipped and he fell into the sea, the weight of his armour sinking him instantly. 'All the barons were much vexed at this misfortune,' observes Froissart philosophically; 'but they were forced to endure it, as they could not in any way rem-edy it.' And, after all, the drowned man had done his adven-turous best to enliven the dreary voyage.

There were few medieval mummers to be found on the road, for the miracle plays were sponsored by the great relig-ious orders, who stood responsible for the performances, and who kept plays and players under their jurisdiction. Year after year at Christmas, at Easter, and on saints' days these devout dramas were repeated to audiences who never wear-ied of the familiar text, nor of the familiar jokes that lent it vivacity. The townspeople and rustics were content to be instructed provided they were also amused, and the element of comedy stood largely responsible for the popularity of the

entertainment. An unfailing source of delight was the shrewishness of wives. The women of the Middle Ages had little
protection from the law, but they were far from being downtrodden. Their masterfulness is everywhere emphasized.
In the Chester cycle the story of the Flood is enlivened by
Noah's domestic difficulties. The 'just and perfect man' sees
trouble ahead when he is bidden to build the Ark ('I pray
my wyffe bee not wrothe when I tell her,' is his anxious
comment); and the event justifies his apprehension. Enter
it she will not, and the close proximity of the beasts has
nothing to do with her determination. The cheap and obvious fun so palatable today is far from the spirit of this
thirteenth-century play, which derives its humour from a
deeper source. Noah's rebellious spouse is a feminist. What
she demands is that her friends shall share her safety:

> I have my gossippes everyone,
> One foot further I will not gone:
> They shall not drowne by Sainte John!
> An' I may save their lyffe.
> They loved me full welle by Christ!
> And, but thou let them in thy chest,
> Rowe nowe, Noah, where thou list,
> And gette thee a new wyffe.

Poor Noah, unable to do her bidding, and aghast at the
situation, can only philosophize, as flouted husbands have
philosophized before and since:

> Lorde, that wemen be crabbed aye,
> And none are meke I dare well saye,
> This is well seene by me to-daye.

Finally, as there is nothing else to be done, his sons ask permission to carry their mother into the Ark; and when he tries to pacify her with a courteous greeting:

> Welckome, wyffe, into this botte!

she deals him a cuff on the head.

> It is good for to be still,

he sadly observes; a sentiment which must have vastly pleased all the husbands and all the wives in the audience.

Even the Nativity plays, acted at Christmas time, present unexpected variants of this chosen theme. In the Coventry cycle, Saint Joseph, being of the House of David, is summoned with others of his kindred as an aspirant to the hand of the Virgin Mary. He is most reluctant to obey, and says in the plainest possible words why he has no wish to marry:

> An old man may never thrive
> With a young wife, so God me save!
> Nay, nay, Sir, let be!
>
> Should I in age begin to dote?
> If I her chide, she will clout my coat,
> As oftentimes we see.

The Towneley *Shepherds' Play*, given under the splendid patronage of the Augustinians, has a singularly beautiful Nativity, prefaced by the simplest and frankest of comedies. It opens with the night watches, the sleeping flocks, the little group of men sitting by the fire, and talking, as such men have always talked, about the hardness of their work and the smallness of their wage. Also, be it remarked, about the peevishness of their wives. They are joined by Mak, a riever, whom they have good cause to mistrust, but whom, being easy tempered and drowsy, they allow to join them. When they fall asleep he arises softly, picks out 'a good fat sheep,' and conveys it to his home. There his spouse, who is every whit as big a thief as he, exercises her wifely prerogative by reproaching him shrilly for his evil ways, which she predicts will bring him to the gallows. Having settled this point, and made good her moral standing, she tries to think of a safe hiding-place for the sheep, and finally decides upon the cradle — empty for the nonce. They will say that she has been delivered of a child.

Soon the shepherds burst into the hut. The wife groans, and Mak entreats them to

> Speke soft
> Over a seke woman's head.

In the pride of paternity he even boasts that he has a lusty boy fit to be the son of a lord. The shepherds search vainly for the lost sheep, and are about to leave when one of them, more gentle-hearted than his fellows, asks leave to kiss the newborn babe. He lifts the counterpane, and the theft is discovered. Mak's wife cries loudly that a foundling has been placed in her baby's cradle; but this goes a step beyond credence. The angry intruders proceed to toss Mak in a blanket until they — or the spectators — weary of the sport, and then return to their flocks. Presently the angel appears and announces the birth of Christ. Angelic hosts sing *Gloria in excelsis Deo*. The shepherds hasten to the stable, adore the divine Child, and proffer their gifts — a bird, a bunch of cherries, and a little ball. The funning is at an end.

There was plenty of horseplay in these simple dramas, and

of that banging about which has always been gratifying to the vuigar. 'It was a pretty part in the Church plays,' wrote Samuel Harsnet, Protestant Bishop of Chichester, 'when the nimble Vice would skip up like a Jack-an-apes on the Devil's neck, and ride him a course, and so belabour him with his wooden dagger "till he made him roar." ' The wooden dagger was in this case an emblem of office, and the 'nimble Vice' who carried it, and who gave his audience all the buffoonery it could reasonably ask, was a species of jester in the Satanic court, a jester, be it said, who held his master in no great awe. The plays were as remote from subtlety as is the modern film; but they were instructive, devout, beautiful in parts, and charged with the flavour of humanity. Occasionally an epicurean line:

A Puddinge may nae man deprave,

evaded asceticism, and spoke volumes for the reasonableness of the day.

The court fool of the Middle Ages was not a sardonic commentator, but a cheerful acrobat who could jump about, turn somersaults, walk on his hands, mimic courtiers, make merry jests, and, when he dared, play rough practical jokes. Hitard, the fool of Edmund Ironside, acquired fame, though what leisure his royal master had to look at him, or listen to him, cannot be conceived. Most kings and princes of the ninth and tenth centuries fought a good deal; but Ironside fought all the time; and fighting did not then mean directing the combat from a safe and convenient hillock. It meant dealing and warding off blows.

Hitard was a jester of parts. After the death of Ironside he made a pilgrimage to Rome, and laid upon the altar of Saint

Peter his deed of gift, conveying Walworth to Canterbury Cathedral, which had been rebuilt by Odo — saint and archbishop — before the year 950. Grandeur was nigh to our human dust when a court fool could play a rôle like this. But in the old town of Senlis, in the church of Saint Maurice, is the stately tomb of another jester, Thévenin de Saint-Ligier, 'Fool of the King our Lord.' The man had honoured the office, and the throne honoured the man.

Professional fools have oftentimes been frowned upon by the great and wise and supercilious. Seneca observed that if a man desired to laugh at folly, he could do no better than scrutinize himself. Christian the First, King of Denmark in the fifteenth century, having been presented with a pair of fools, declined their services. He said that if he wanted folly, his courtiers could supply his needs. But the men of the Middle Ages were less cynical because less egotistical. Self-analysis played little part in their development. What they valued in a fool was the ready and recognizable joke at which they could freely laugh. Saint Louis, one of the wisest of his order, so relished this fun-making that often, when it was proposed to read some pious chronicle, he postponed being edified until after he had been amused. 'There is no book so good when one has dined,' he said, 'as gay talk and a merry jest.' Charles the Fifth of France, called 'the Wise,' had several fools with whom he exchanged '*paroles joyeuses et honnestes*' between the hours of Mass and Council.

The popularity of court fools increased rather than diminished during the fifteenth and sixteenth centuries. Cardinal Wolsey presented his own fool, Patch, to Henry the Eighth, greatly to the King's delight and to Patch's discomfiture. John Heywood, jester, dramatist, and scholar, survived

Henry, and young Edward the Sixth, who joked very little, and Queen Mary, who — so says Sir Frederic Madden — 'was of a cultivated intelligence and fond of innocent fun.' Heywood could do more than jest. He made a Latin oration at the Queen's wedding. Men were then trained to listen to Latin orations. It speaks volumes for the discipline of a court.

Tarleton, a very accomplished fool, played a nervous and jumpy part in the reign of Elizabeth; and James the First had a brother fool, Archie Armstrong, who was the most famous of his kind. 'Salt Archie' he was called, and the epithet suited him well. His wit was keen, and he had the pitilessness of a hard and acquisitive nature. He accompanied the Prince of Wales and Buckingham on their memorable journey to Spain, to seek the hand of the Infanta; and he actually succeeded in worming a pension — which was paid — from Philip the Fourth. In the end he grew too outrageous to be endured. His enemies multiplied, and he was dismissed from office with much pomp and ceremony. His jester's coat was 'pulled over his head' in the presence of the King (Charles the First had succeeded James), Buckingham, Archbishop Laud, and 'other great lords of the Council,' all of whom he had seriously affronted. A gentleman who saw him in sober black asked him what had become of his fool's coat. 'My Lord of Canterbury hath taken it from me,' was the answer, 'because either he or the Scots Bishops have the use of it themselves.' Which proves that 'Salt Archie' had lost none of his Attic qualities. A contemporary chronicler says that he was compelled to spend the rest of his days in harassing his creditors and increasing his fortune, which may have been a congenial occupation, but which makes a poor showing by the side of Hitard's splendid gesture.

22

It is something of a surprise to learn that the minstrel of the Middle Ages was not a musician only, but an acrobat and juggler as well. He could 'jump high,' 'leap through hoops,' and 'throw and catch apples on two knives.' One of the order makes proud boast of his accomplishments:

> I am a minstrel of the viol,
> I know the musette and the flute,
> And the chants of the priests,
> And the speech of chivalry.
> I know how to use the juggler's cup,
> And make the snail appear
> Alive and leaping on the table.

The unwonted nimbleness of the snail must have been the high light of this entertainment, which otherwise was common enough. De Joinville tells us that three Armenian minstrels, who had made a pilgrimage to the Holy Land, came to the court of Saint Louis. They played on their trumpets with piercing sweetness 'marvellous to hear,' and they were graceful acrobats. 'A towel was put under their feet, and, holding themselves erect and rigid, they turned complete somersaults, landing with their feet on the little towel.'

The King took more pleasure in minstrels than in jesters. He rewarded them generously, and, like the kind Lady of Buccleuch, he gave shelter to such as were too old and feeble to wander through the land. There is something very charming about the amenities of Saint Louis's court. A wise, quaint, sober, humorous man who liked frank intercourse with his friends. Being concerned about the welfare of their souls, he was wont to ask them whether they would not rather be lepers than commit a mortal sin. As good courtiers, eager to please a good king, they always professed a devout preference for leprosy. Then one day he put the question to the Lord de Joinville. 'Sire,' was the answer, 'I would rather commit thirty mortal sins than be a leper.' Louis let it pass. He knew de Joinville's worth, and he understood *la vertu moyenne*, that average rectitude which human nature has never signally lacked, and which, if it fails to make this the best of all possible worlds, saves it from being the worst.

A comprehension of this truth pervades the chronicles of the Middle Ages, the stories, poems, legends, and jests that have come down to us undisturbed, but often very disturbing. It was a simpler matter to write history then than now, but it was not easy. Matthew Prior, monk of Saint Albans, and greatest of thirteenth-century chroniclers, said that the task of the historian was a hard one, for if he told the truth he offended man, and if he told what was false he offended God. Truth and falsehood being interlaced, it was well to compromise as Philippe de Comines compromised two centuries later. 'Our good master, Louis the Eleventh, whom God pardon,' he wrote piously, with a clear understanding of mortal man and of the hearts of kings.

It is not only the laugh which bubbles up from the misrepresented pages of medieval life that makes that life so plain to us. Warmth and simplicity, courage and homeliness, illuminate its outlines. Froissart tells us that when the Black Prince held court in Gascony, it was the abode of 'all nobleness, joy and jollity, all largesse, gentleness and honour.' That, of course, was the happy fate (as long as it lasted) of the great and powerful. But in the same century the Swiss Federation, representing men of all classes, signed this solemn pledge: 'We engage to assist one another with our lives and fortunes against all who shall in any way attempt to injure us in our honour, prosperity, or freedom.' And again, in the same century, the servant-maids of Troyes, as obstinately proud of their usefulness as if they had been knights or men-at-arms, presented to the Church of Saint Mary Magdalen a beautifully carved and deftly coloured statue of their patroness, Saint Martha. There it stood to represent their honourable labour, which was highly esteemed, and had, like the labour of the hard-worked apprentices, its special rights and privileges.

Now and then a cheerful chronicler like M. Jusserand turns from Cathedrals to ale houses, and from dungeons and torture chambers to characteristic village legislature. He tells us, for example, that in 1364 one John Penrose, a publican of Middlesex, was found guilty of watering his wine; for which offence he was condemned to stand in the pillory, to drink all of the adulterated wine he could hold (no question here of the dreadful water torture), and to have the rest of it poured over his head. An ingenious penalty designed to fit the crime, and to provide entertainment for the customers he had defrauded. Penrose's misdeed was a trivial one, but it was more common than high treason, and of far more concern to his neighbours.

Cheating in one form or another has always been the prevailing sin of humanity. If there were only two men left in the world, there would still be a chance and an inducement to cheat. The people of Hamelin cheated the Pied Piper, and lost their children in consequence. The laugh was on the cheaters. Reineche Fuchs cheated all his associates successfully and finally. The laugh was on the cheated. There was sure to be a laugh, but there was no certainty that it would be rightly directed. What hero of the Middle Ages was more magnificent than the Cid? What soldier won so many pitched battles? What champion of Christendom stood so invincibly against the encroachments of the infidels? A wise man, too; witness his counsel to his wife before leaving her for the wars: 'Lay aside thy silken raiment until my return, for wives should dress plainly in their husbands' absence; and show my letters to no one, not to thy nearest of kin, lest, reading them, they guess rightly at things they do not know.'

Yet this superb Castilian is credited by the unknown poet who tells his tale in the oldest of Spanish verse with a piece of trickery as shameless as any devised by Reynard or the Master Thief. Being sorely in need of money to pay his soldiers, he fills two coffers with sand, covering them with fine scarlet leather, and studding them richly with gold nails. These he offers through his squire, Antolinez, to the Jew money-lenders of Burgos as security for a loan of six hundred marks. Antolinez declares that they are filled with Moorish gold and treasure which will become the property of the usurers if the money be not returned within a year, but that they must not be opened in the meantime. This unlikely statement is accepted on the word of a soldier. The six hundred marks are advanced, and the Jews, happy in anticipation of a good bargain, burst into praise of Spain's great champion: 'Blest be the hour, oh warrior, when you first girded sword to your side!' The shameless squire winds up the business by asking and receiving a commission as a reward for his services. The laugh is on the cheated; and the episode is told with a simplicity and candour which we cannot hope to emulate.

As a matter of fact, it is hard for us to be simple and candid because we are never genuinely unconcerned. A passion for readjustment is necessarily the passion of a sentimental, radical, and reforming age. Three medieval stories, all well known and widely popular, have come down to us today: the thirteenth-century story of the Piper of Hamelin, the fourteenth-century story of Tyl Eulenspiegel, and the twelfth-century story of Reineche Fuchs. The first is a highly dramatic tale of retributive justice; the second a recital of pure mischief, the kind of mischief which Mrs. Pennell found so keenly illustrative of the Middle Ages; the third a triumphant glorification of rascality, the most unmoral narrative ever told the world.

Now what sea changes have these stories suffered at the hands of a serious generation, and what may happen to them in the future? Browning, indeed, dealt with the Piper in his happiest vein — vivid, humorous, cynical, sympathetic (even to the poor disregarded rats), and with only four lines of moral tacked to the end of his poem. It was left for Josephine Preston Peabody to infuse into her dramatic version of the tale a twentieth-century atmosphere as remote from its original setting as Chicago's Century of Progress is remote from the Cotswold Games or the Council of Trent. Her Piper is primarily a reformer. He takes the children from their parents because these parents are unworthy of their office. He keeps them because he loves them (all of them, apparently) without stint. He surrenders them because his reawakened conscience tells him that this is the proper thing for him to do. In the interval he plays the part of knight errant, is smitten to the heart when he learns that the Burgomeister's daughter is about to enter a nunnery (a circumstance which would have awakened no concern in the year 1284), and promptly rescues her from being

> shut away
> Out of the light,

which is his simple conception of a convent life. It is not for the modern playwright to bridge the chasm between our world and the logical and laughing world which held that Hamelin town got no more than it deserved.

With Tyl Eulenspiegel we leave the unrestricted realm of legend for the half lights of tradition. There probably was a peasant-born Brunswick jester of that name who was always up to mischief, who hated townspeople because he was country bred, and innkeepers and tradesmen because they presented him with bills, and priests and princes because they curbed his lawlessness. The popular chap-book which bore his name was written after his death by Thomas Mürner, who might have been better employed. It is scurrilous, indecent, and heavy-handed, destitute of wit, but crammed full of the rough practical jokes which are laughter-provoking to the sluggish mind. Thanks to its unsavoury pages, the memory of Tyl Eulenspiegel's pranks lingered in the German countryside, became familiar to the Netherlands, and passed over to England, where they were ascribed to a mythical scamp called Howleglass, a figure by no means heroic, but less brutal and obscene than his German prototype.

There does not seem to be much material here for modernization. It will be remembered that the Russian ballet borrowed Tyl, and dealt with him after the fashion of ballets. There was at least a suggestion of laughter in its grotesque exaggerations, in the apparent hilarity of the dancers, and in the unrestrained mirthfulness of the music. The audience might have broken into happy smiles if it had not been trying so hard to decipher the meaning of the crowded scenes and complicated pantomime.

But why should Charles de Coster have chosen this unscrupulous rogue as the hero of his 'Légend d'Ulenspiegel'? Why should he have transformed him into a Flemish patriot whose animating motive is hatred of that calumniated king, Philip the Second, a king who, by the way, was born nearly two centuries after the Brunswick jester's death. In de Coster's 'Légend' Tyl's father, Claes, is burnt at the stake for heresy, a happening not unknown elsewhere. 'You are burnt for heresy,' observes Augustine Birrell with philosophic calm. 'That is right enough. No one would complain of that.' Apparently Tyl did complain, for he carries a handful of his father's ashes in a bag hung around his neck, a dramatic touch which does not lend itself to comedy. When he cries 'My father's ashes beat against my heart!' he is as much like the original Eulenspiegel as William Tell is like Grimaldi, or as the nineteenth century is like the fourteenth. We cannot make merry over heresy, and the stake, and parental ashes in a bag.

There are no weak concessions to merriment in the twentieth-century play 'Tyl Ulenspiegel,' by Mr. Ashley Dukes. It ignores the chap-book, and follows the Flemish story, with an added weight of polemical and political arguments, well set forth, but not distinctly diverting. Tyl's noble animosity has been transferred from Philip to Alva — another safe target. Even the good little Nele, his sweetheart, dreams of playing the rôle of Judith, and laboriously learns

29

the viol that she may charm — and slay — the great soldier.
She says encouragingly of her lover, 'He runs in cap and
bells'; but we catch no glimpse of the cap, and hear no echo
of the bells. The one joke, recognizable as such, is made by
the gallant lieutenant: 'I will brave all dangers but marriage.' The one comic episode is the descent of Tyl and his
friend, Lamme, through the chimney of the inn when they
might have come in by the door. The well-written play,
full of action and variety, is a notable example of what happens when a medieval story is modernized. A great deal that
is thoughtful and discursive is added to its somewhat meagre
outlines; but the ready laughter of the Middle Ages is un-
avoidably left out. It has slumbered for five epoch-making
centuries, and might sound unauthorized in our ears.

Certainly unauthorized when it comes to the third story,
'Reineche Fuchs,' which has not a moral leg to stand on.
Nobody has yet been able to make of Reynard a reformer, a
philanthropist, or a patriot. His enormous popularity has
disposed critics to treat him with unwarranted and mislead-
ing respect. His history has been pronounced — in Germany — to be the best book in the world next to the Bible;
a distinction which it shares with some thousands of masterpieces in every land. It has also been called the most profoundly humorous book ever written; but it lacks the keenness with which the humourist turns a knave's knavery into
a weapon of self-destruction, directed by the watchful and
highly humorous gods. Serious-minded readers see in it a
satire against Church and State, preferably the former; but
serious-minded readers have seen well-directed satire in
'Mother Goose,' and are capable of seeing it in Lear's 'Book
of Nonsense.'

30

Of course the beasts — and birds — are men. Chanticleer might at any moment make a Fourth of July speech over the radio. Reynard's farewell address before starting on his pilgrimage to Rome might be printed — with modified spelling — in the Church news. 'I shal not reste by night nor day til I bee assoylled,' he says with noble enthusiasm; and asks the prayers of all his old associates. 'They said that they alle wold remembre him.' The lion, deeply edified, gives him Bellyn the ram and Kywart the hare as companions; a circumstance which induces him to turn aside on his journey, and conduct Kywart to his castle of Maleperduys that he may see his affectionate Aunt Ermelyn. There the helpless animal is promptly slain, and the whole fox family (Ermelyn does her duty by her husband) feast happily, 'for Kywart had a good fat body.'

Reynard's reasons for abandoning his pilgrimage are as admirable as his reasons for going on it. He reflects, truthfully enough, 'There is in the world many a good man who has never been to Rome,' and decides to be one of these good men. His decision is couched in words which would have won favour with 'Piers Plowman': 'I mean to take my way home, and I shall earn my bread honestly and aid the poor.' So having fooled everybody, from the 'fair and sorrowful hens' who mourn their dead sister to Bruin the bear, and Isengrin the lordly wolf, and Sir Tybert the cat, who should have known better, he retires, by favour of the sorely cheated lion, to Maleperduys and Dame Ermelyn, and his promising brood of foxlings, with whom 'he lyved forthon in grete joy and gladness.' So, it will be remembered, did the Master Thief.

Reynard, like Gulliver, is as pleasing to the child as to the adult, children being by nature pitiless and unmoral. The robust nurseries of the sixties and seventies held him in high esteem. With the help of the 'Arabian Nights' and 'Popular Tales from the Norse' he counteracted the influence of Miss Edgeworth and 'Sandford and Merton.' The vivid and highly coloured pictures which illustrated his career lent emphasis to the tale. Indeed poor Kywart, terror-stricken and flattened to earth when the fox springs upon him, brandishing in mockery his pilgrim's staff, could not be looked at comfortably. Hannah More objected to Scott's poems because they lacked 'practical precept.' One wonders if 'Reineche Fuchs' was part of her childhood's lore.

Other medieval stories have come trailing down to us, suffering strange mutations on the way. Griselda the patient, who slipped from Italy to England, and in Chaucer's hands became the heroine of one of the loveliest tales ever told the world, degenerated during the centuries into the perfect wife who won renown and wealth by saying on all occasions and under all provocations: 'What the gudeman does is right'; or into the still more unaccountable lady who maintained that a mare was a cow because her husband said so. It would seem as though men, suffering from shrewish wives, evolved this type of woman to gratify the unsatisfied instincts of their souls.

Sigrid Undset has said truly that intelligent moderns show 'an amazing incapacity to understand the men and women of the Middle Ages.' Yet she who knows so much about them has never heard them laugh. And what has she lost if her profoundly serious soul has missed this characteristic note! She has far more to say about abbots and archbishops than about the common people; but the cloister was by no means a cheerless place.

> I read and teach and laugh and pray,
> And, snoring, sleep,

writes an Irish monk of the eleventh century who knew when he was well off, and expressed his satisfaction in creditable Latin verse. The twelfth-century Abbot of Bourgeuil must have had a pleasant and rather modern sense of humour when he said that he had been compelled by some magic spell to lend his Ovid to a friend. In his right mind he would have never done such a thing, knowing well that it would not be returned to him.

Four light-hearted verses by a nameless Irish scholar of the tenth century (when there were scholars and scholarship in Ireland) reflect the temperament of the Celtic man of letters. They were written in Latin, were turned into English by Mr. Robin Flower, and are quoted by that lover of scholarship, Miss Helen Waddell:

> I and Pangur Ban, my cat,
> 'Tis a like task we are at;
> Hunting mice is his delight,
> Hunting words I sit all night.
>
> 'Tis a merry thing to see
> At our tasks how glad are we,
> When at home we sit and find
> Entertainment to our mind.
>
> 'Gainst the wall he sets his eye,
> Full and fierce and sharp and sly;

33

'Gainst the wall of knowledge, I
All my little wisdom try.

So in peace our tasks we ply,
Pangur Ban, my cat, and I;
In our arts we find our bliss,
I have mine and he has his.

Can it be that six hundred years divide this philosophic
Irish student from the philosophic and studious Montaigne,
and Pangur Ban from Montaigne's cat, who sported with
his master on terms of perfect equality?

II

THE SILENCING OF LAUGHTER

England has never been merry England since everybody learned to read.

ANDREW LANG

II

THE SILENCING OF LAUGHTER

IF ILLITERACY be sufficient to ensure cheerfulness, then Elizabeth's England has a right to be called, as it always is called, 'merry.' When people say 'merry England,' they refer, as a rule, to her great and glorious reign. They have Spenser's warrant for so doing:

Saint George of merry England, the sign of victoree.

When Sir Edward German wrote a gay little opera which has been successfully revived, and called it 'Merrie England,' the audience expected to see, and did see, the court of the Virgin Queen. It was not a merry court (merry courts have been few and far between), and the land it dominated was not a merry land; but reading and writing cannot be held responsible for its uneasiness. We have Sir Thomas More's word for it that in his day one half of England's inhabitants were unacquainted with their letters; and the disturbing march of education had gone but a little way in the succeeding half century. If Judith Shakespeare could not sign her name, we have no reason to suppose that universal book learning — unkindly deprecated by Mr. Lang — was sowing the seeds of unrest.

We are so dazzled by the glory of Elizabeth's England that

we never look beyond the row of glittering names. We rightly consider that a country that had Shakespeare had enough. The greatest possession in the world was hers, and hers to keep. She had also the most perfect possession in the world, Sir Philip Sidney. She had a battered little ship called the *Golden Hind*, which was the first English vessel to circumnavigate the world, and which was carefully preserved as a monument to the greatest mariner in the world, Sir Francis Drake. She had statesmen as astute and as unscrupulous as any on earth; and she had gentlemen adventurers more brave and more unscrupulous than any on the seas. She had the first public theatre ever built in London, and she had great plays acted on its boards. She had natural loveliness unsurpassed and unpolluted — 'the garden of God,' said John Speed. She had even the precious boon, tobacco, though she did not fully understand the value of the gift. She had much that was better worth having than laughter; but she did not laugh spontaneously, and she had already begun the serious cultivation of mirth. The 'Hundred Merry Tales,' dull enough for the most part, represent an earnest endeavour to promote that hilarity which the Middle Ages had vainly striven to suppress.

There was peace in the land. Or, at least, there was no war to sap the country's strength. 'We Englishmen live in security,' wrote Walsingham, 'grounding our quietness on others' harms.' But this quietness was shot through with tragic happenings (the loss of young Marlowe in a tavern brawl, the sadness of Spenser's deathbed), and with a bitter current of discontent. Barnabe Rich said that the poor were too poor, and that no one cared 'for such as were in want.' His words were borne out by Nicholas Breton, a cheerful

soul not given to repining, but none the less a close observer
of his day. It was his opinion that poverty, once esteemed
as the child of Heaven, was wearing the garments of dis-
grace, and that 'the honest poor man' was having a hard
time of it. 'He is a stranger in the world, for no man craves
his acquaintance, and his funeral is without ceremony when
there is no mourning for the miss of him.' Thomas Nash
observed the growing ill-will between the classes. 'The
courtier disdaineth the citizen, the citizen the countryman,
the shoemaker the cobbler.' England was growing rich on
wool; but the sheep were grazing on what had once been
arable land, and the ploughman paid the price of prosperity. So did the petty consumer.

> The more sheep, the dearer is the corn,
> The more sheep, the fewer eggs to the penny,

expressed his view of the situation.

Above all, there was an ever-darkening quarrel over
creeds, an ever-deepening distrust of neighbour for neighbour. 'Reineche Fuchs' was to be had in its English text by
all disposed to laughter; but it was not so popular as 'The
Hunter of the Romish Fox,' the title of which sufficiently
indicated the bellicose nature of its contents. 'The Bailiff's
Daughter of Islington' was a popular, cheerful, and not too
sensible ballad; but by its side might be seen 'The Lamenta-
tion of a Damned Soul,' which sounds like an advance
guard of Wesleyan literature. England did not waste her
strength on civil wars and call them religious, as did France;
or expend on polemical disputes the energy which should
have gone into colonization, as did Germany; but she
fussed and fumed, passed savage laws, and saw them defied

by her worthiest sons. The Jesuit priest went to his hideous death, protesting his loyalty to the Crown. The Puritan whose right hand had been chopped off raised his bleeding stump, and cried, 'God save the Queen!' But the priest had a successor ready to take up his work, and the Puritan went his way, protesting when he felt it his duty to protest. Both were unconquerable, and neither was provocative of laughter.

The dissolution of the guilds, which went hand in hand with the dissolution of the monasteries, was responsible for the extreme poverty of the people. The monasteries themselves were sorely missed. No one pretends that the greedy courtiers who got possession of the Church estates made as good landlords as the monks had made. And with the monasteries went the rural 'hospitals,' most of which were simply almshouses, harbouring the maimed and helpless. Their inmates were turned into the roads, to beg, or steal, or die. From one such shelter a hundred blind men were cast out with no provision for their future. The artisan and the labourer were not much better off than was the beggar, for the loss of their guilds — 'stripped,' says Augustus Jessopp, 'of their last farthing, their last rag and cup and platter' — meant the loss of all that had ensured them the reward of labour.

Dr. James Walsh corroborates Mr. Jessopp's statement that there were no less than thirty thousand of these guilds in pre-Reformation England. They had reached their highest development in that golden age of craftsmanship, the thirteenth century; and they represented democracy in its best and sanest aspect. Beginning as beneficial societies, they showed what could be done by self help and organization; and they became the great educators in every field of work. It was the guilds that ruled the important and turbulent world of apprenticeship; the guilds that lent money, settled disputes, ensured against fire and other calamities, regulated hours of labour (seven, eight, or nine hours a day for artisans), and gave every year great feasts, 'designed to promote love and amity and good communication for the several weal of the fraternity.' Tankards of ale were given to the poor on these occasions, and as much as thirty pence was paid to the minstrels who made music for the banqueters. The guilds did for the workmen of the thirteenth century all that the trade-unions do for the workmen of the twentieth century, and a great deal more, for they fostered the best possible production, the highest personal achievement. The medieval craftsman who spent long and loving weeks over the lock, key, and hinges of a sacristy chest was sure of his wages and of intelligent understanding. There was room in his life for pride as well as for bodily comfort.

Mr. Jessopp, who looked back upon the lost guilds with the deep regard of an antiquarian, mourned for them as if he had been a sixteenth-century priest rather than a nineteenth-century parson. He did not even take comfort in the thought that a few powerful companies like the merchant tailors, the goldsmiths, and the stationers survived the Reformation by pleading their purely secular character. Nine tenths of the guilds were too closely associated with the Church and with the monasteries to escape destruction when they had funds and property worth seizing; and this universal confiscation reduced to uttermost poverty thousands of English workingmen. The increase of destitution paved the way for the Tudor poor-laws, first of their kind, which at their best may be described as codes for badgering the indigent, and at their worst as statutes for the persecution of the unhappy. An act passed in the reign of Edward the Sixth has been described as written in letters of blood. It aimed at sweeping out of sight all the unfortunates who had been beggared in his father's reign, as well as the less miserable creatures who had never owned anything to lose. Both classes were set down as vagabonds. If they were rude handicraftsmen, they were forbidden to work. If they were petty tradesmen, they were forbidden to sell. 'Tynkers, pedlars, and such like vagrant personnes are more hurtfull than necessarie to the Common Wealth of this realme,' said the act, and this was doubtless true. But the tinker and the pedlar were trying to live, because there had come down to them from happier ages a belief that life was good.

The statutes of Elizabeth's day went much further than any which had preceded them. An 'Acte for the punishment of vagabonds' would have driven Autolycus into hiding. Not only 'all pedlars, tynkers, and petye chapmen,' but 'all scollers of the Universities of Oxford or Cambridge who goe about begginge'; not only 'ydle personnes fayninge to have knowledge of phisnomye and palmestrye,' but 'jugglers, fencers, bearwardes, common players in interludes, and minstrels not belonging to any baron of this realme,' were classed together as rogues and vagabonds, and handed over to the courts, thereby extinguishing much laughter in England.

The law was doubtless disobeyed. Any law forbidding Englishmen to roam was disobeyed. They could not be kept in one spot when they wanted to move on. Rural records in Tudor days present a monotonous narrative of wayfarers apprehended, whipped, and returned to their own parishes, which did not welcome them, and where they would not stay. There was no taint of serfdom in their blood. The earth beneath their feet and the cloud-flecked sky overhead were their inheritance. They would go where they listed. They would be 'masterless men,' subject as such to harsh penalties, but part and parcel of the age-old revolt against despotism — a revolt which had the wandering tinker at one end of the line, and the barons of Runnymede at the other.

There were kind Christians and worthy citizens in Elizabeth's day, as there were before and after; but they could do little to stem the general distress. The hospital at Greenwich was rebuilt by that 'goodly good gentleman,' William Lambarde. The almshouses founded by Lord Burleigh at Stamford still stand. They sheltered thirteen poor men, and the almshouses erected at Aldenham by the brewer, Richard Platt, held the same number. Thomas Cuttell left a fund to provide one good dinner a year for the prisoners at Newgate, which was a kindly deed. Sir Martin Bowes, a London alderman, left money for the repairing of the city's neglected conduits. Elizabeth Gavener of Devon bequeathed her manor of Shalcombe to be sold, and the proceeds devoted to the repairing of the equally neglected highways.

All this was work well done, and historians have made much of it. But thirteen paupers sitting down to their daily dinners meant nothing to the hordes of dinnerless men who skulked and hid and stole and died, unhindered and unhelped. Beg they dared not, for even licensed beggars who wore a badge to proclaim their privilege were permitted to solicit alms in their own parishes and no other. They no longer went 'light-heart and gay' wherever their fancy led them. Fletcher, indeed, wrote a play called 'The Beggar's Bush' which had a cheerful beggars' song; but he discreetly located it in the Netherlands, where, for all he knew, these 'children of idleness whose lives are a resolution of ease' might go singing and whistling on the highways.

A less merry sight met the eyes of Lord Howard, admiral of the Queen's fleet, when he beheld his seamen sick, penniless, and starving in the streets of Margate. Elizabeth could not be induced to pay or feed her soldiers and sailors. 'It was not that the commissariat broke down,' says Gordon Goodwin. 'There was no commissariat.' She honestly believed and said that if her subjects were loyal to her, they should be ready to defend her 'at their own charges'; a point of view intelligible in a Highland chieftain who gathers his clan about him, but not in the sovereign of a great nation. 'When England was thrilling with its triumph over the Armada,' says the historian, Green, 'the Queen was grumbling at the cost, and making her profit out of the spoiled provisions she had ordered for the fleet that saved her.'

Miserliness is the one vice that grows stronger with increasing years. It yields its sordid pleasures to the end. What had been thrift in Elizabeth's middle age became an overmastering passion before she died. Her soldiers for foreign service were taken from the prisons, and picked up by press gangs. 'Loose and runaway men' were gathered in and jailed until they could be shipped to the Low Countries. Easter Sunday offered a magnificent chance for stratagem, for on that day everyone was legally bound to take the sacrament. The press gangs surrounded the parish

44

churches, and seized the younger men. Unless they were handsomely redeemed they were sent across the sea to be shot, or die of fever, or be returned wasted with disease. The system was not always so economical as it seemed. In the spring of 1563 there were despatched to Havre 'cut-purses, horse-stealers, and highwaymen,' with a sprinkling of old soldiers to leaven the mass. It mattered little of what material these troops were made, for the plague was waiting for them, and by midsummer was taking a toll of sixty men a day. Havre was surrendered, and a remnant of its garrison returned to Portsmouth in August. There was no quarantine and no provision made for their reception. They scattered to their homes, carrying disease with them. Where hundreds had died in France, thousands died in England; and London, which had deemed itself safe, suffered the heaviest loss.

Twenty-five years later the destruction of the Armada was the burden of exultant song and story; but there were those who took little pride in the part that England played. Every one knows about Drake and his game of bowls; but how many of us hear Leicester testify that the four thousand recruits who assembled at Tilbury found not so much as a loaf of bread or a draught of beer on which to break their fast? How many hear Howard's appeal: 'For the love of God send us powder and shot!' or his sad admission that, while the ships despatched by cities and citizens were well fitted out, those sent at the expense of the crown lacked 'the barest necessities'? Above all, how many hear Walsingham's heartbroken cry: 'The Queen's parsimony at home hath bereaved us of the famousest victory that ever our nation had at sea.' It was a great and glorious reign, but

merry it was not. Compared to the penniless seamen of
Margate, the medieval herbalists led a pleasant life. Compared to the 'begging poor' who were permitted to ask for
alms, and the 'vagabond' poor who were expected to starve
in silence, the medieval 'toth-drawers' and needle-sellers
were free and happy men. When we are listening for
laughter, it is not on the Queen's highways that we may
hope to hear it.

Yet her subjects were never without their simple pleasures.
They had the Cotswold games. They had their May queen
as of yore, and at Christmas time their Lord of Misrule,
who made no trouble because he no longer ruled. He was
merely carried into church when the service was over and
carried out again. They had bears to bait. Every township
kept a bear for this laudable purpose. We are told that
one petty borough which had the misfortune to lose its
bear sold the church Bible to buy another. Villages too poor
to afford a bear were perforce content with humbler sports.
A cat hung up in a leather bag as a target for crossbows,
or a cock in an earthenware vessel to be stoned, or a few
doves to be 'sealed' (blinded) for the sake of their strange,
disordered flight.

Now and then a witch was done to death by a too strenu-
ous mob; but this was a diversion hard to come by, and
receiving no encouragement from authority. Elizabeth's
firm intelligence was well-nigh superstition-proof. Her
successor acquired fame as a foe to witchcraft; but he had
been bred in Scotland, and the English witches were poor
feckless things compared to their terrible Scottish sisters.
It is true that in 1560 Bishop Jewel, freshly appointed to
the see of Salisbury, besought the Queen to enforce the laws

against witchcraft, which had fallen into disuse. He drew an agitated picture of the evils which had resulted from her leniency, of a hapless people unprotected from the power that works in darkness. 'Your Grace's subjects pine away even unto death. Their colour fadeth, their flesh rotteth, their speech is benumbed, their senses are bereft.'

This was good measure on Satan's part; but the recountal carried no conviction to Elizabeth, though she was ready to take mild measures of precaution. When a waxen figure was picked up in Lincoln's Inn-fields, and pronounced to be her own image and likeness, she sent for her astrologer, Dr. John Dee, and bade him counteract its malice. She made the same use of the learned gentleman when she had the toothache, being actuated in both cases by a desire to get all the good she could out of a salaried official. She no more feared injury to English constitutions from witchcraft than she feared injury to English ethics from playing cards. Henry the Eighth, who had a tender regard for the morality of his subjects, restricted the sale of cards; but his daughter was less austere. She held them to be a commendable amusement for such as bad weather kept indoors.

In all this there was much sense, but little mirth. Where the medieval observers had laughed, the Elizabethans too often berated. The shrewishness of wives, the wilfulness of women, were no laughing matter to John Stubbs, who said that they beggared their husbands by their extravagance, and cared not who paid for their finery. It was no laughing matter to Thomas Dekker, who conceived that English husbands were ill-treated by their wives, and whose satire has an angry edge. To be ruined by wastefulness was no worse than to be mastered by ill-temper; and the folly of women who 'diet their faces,' and 'ensparkle their eyes with spiritualized distillations,' incited him to loud contempt. Only Nicholas Breton reproduced the medieval atmosphere in his story of the wife who devoured the great eel which her husband was fattening as a gift for his landlord. The serving-maid, 'who had wit enough to make a fool of a tame goose,' adroitly suggests to the angry man that her mistress is perhaps breeding, which would account for her inordinate appetite; and that she may bear him a fine boy worth many bushels of eels. The poor simpleton looks at his gluttonous helpmate sitting heavily in her chair, and his heart is softened. Gently he approaches her, patiently he listens to the 'home complaints' which she has all ready for him, and gratefully he accepts the next morning a small portion of what is left of the eel pie. It is a perfect picture of domestic life, undisturbed by any hint of reprobation.

The curious thing about the situation was the defenceless-ness of women under the law. An Antwerp merchant who visited England in 1579, and who pronounced it to be 'the female Paradise,' was amazed and amused by the fact that English wives were 'entirely in the power of their husbands, life only excepted.' A man might not kill his wife or sell her. He occasionally did one or the other, but the act was illegal. For the rest she belonged to him as did his dog or his horse; but she was far from emulating the submissiveness of these useful animals. She lorded it over her household at home, and was treated with deference abroad. 'At all banquets and feasts she is shown the great-est honour, is placed at the upper end of the table and is served first.' Women of the well-to-do class led an easy life, 'visiting their gossips and being diverted thereby.'

Women of the lower class forgathered in taverns and pot-houses to tipple. This had been their reprehensible custom before Elizabeth's day; and — to their shame be it spoken — they paid their score, if need be, with their yokemates' belongings:

> One bringeth her husband's hood,
> Because the ale is good;
> Another bringeth his cap
> To offer to the ale tap.

Skelton was disposed to lay the blame for women's outrageous behaviour upon Chaucer, inasmuch as the Wife of Bath had taught them that the one thing desirable was sovereignty over their husbands, and that in this sovereignty alone lay all chance of marital content. But Chaucer counteracted the Wife's tale with the Clerk's tale of Griselda the patient. In Elizabeth's day patience, or at least obedience, was out of date. A popular song hawked about the streets had for a title 'God Send Me a Wife that Will Do as I Say!' and another exalted the carefree life of the bachelor:

> Married men may sit and groan;
> He is content and letteth well alone.

The Queen herself was not safe from reproach, being of a most wilful and changeable disposition, and wholly lacking in the royal virtue of punctuality. A pleasant tale is told of her removal from Windsor to London. The wagon train (she was weightily burdened with luggage) was ordered to be in readiness. Three days running it waited for its rich loads, and three days running she postponed her departure. When on the third day the master carter was informed of this fact, he swore lustily. 'Now I know,' he said, 'that the Queen is just such another as my wife.' From an open window overhead came an angry laugh. Then a messenger brought him a gold angel. Her Majesty had overheard, and had sent it to stop his mouth. The Tudors were never deficient in humour.

Elizabeth's progresses throughout her kingdom awakened enthusiasm when her reign was young, and became a grievous tax upon her subjects when she had outworn her welcome at their doors. She liked being entertained at their expense, and she liked it better and better as they grew more unwilling, or perhaps more unable, to entertain her. Her second visit to Oxford in 1592 occasioned as little merriment as the memorable visit of George the Third in 1786. Her court, once brilliant, always dignified, but never gay, grew insufferably tedious as the years went by. Men were men then as before and since. Some of them wanted mistresses, many of them wanted wives. They gratified both inclinations, but at the risk of losing the royal favour. They were ambitious then as before and since. Even in the matter of wedlock, ambition played its part. They sought well-dowered brides, or, better still, influential fathers-in-law. Sully was not the only courtier in Europe who expressed his profound conviction that the really important element in marriage was a father-in-law.

Married or single, they grew reasonably tired of pretending that the mere presence of the Queen was enough to satisfy all ardent emotions, and dispel all mutinous desires. When there was hope in a great lord's heart that she would marry a subject, and that he might be her choice, ambition flared high. As that hope faded, there was nothing to re-

EASTERN DISTRICT HIGH SCHOOL
127 Marcy Avenue—Brooklyn, N. Y.

place it. For years they watched her amorous antics with the Duc d'Alençon, and derived what entertainment they could from that mockery of courtship. For years they saw their strong-stomached sovereign fondle and caress the hideous little creature for whom she professed a tender regard, and to whom she wrote amorous letters which failed to deceive his clear-sighted, cold-hearted mother. Not being in the habit of truth-telling, Catherine de Médicis was never at the mercy of a lie.

The hope of enrichment at Elizabeth's hands was as futile as the hope of marriage. Her purse-strings were drawn tight, her grants were few and far between. Leicester was the sole recipient of her bounty; and when he died, she seized upon his estate and sold it to repay his debts to the exchequer. Burleigh, her faithful minister, and twelve times her host, never grew rich; Walsingham and Hatton died insolvent. It was understood that the Queen did not give money, she received it. A purse filled with gold pieces was an acceptable offering from any gentleman of her court. On New Year's Day, 1578, she took in — to her vast pleasure and contentment — the sum of nine hundred and ninety-three pounds and thirteen shillings. It was customary for the bishops to send her from ten to twenty pounds, which was as little as they could do, seeing that if they died their incomes went to the Crown until their successors were appointed. Elizabeth's devotion to the Church of which she was the head may be measured by the fact that Wells did without a bishop for ten years, Ely for eighteen years, and Oxford for forty-one. The famous remark of a devout but profane Episcopalian, 'Who in Hell will confirm us?' would have been appropriate to this singular situation.

8897

Thirty-three years ago Mr. Owen Seaman wrote some characteristic verses in praise of Queen Elizabeth's England. He said nothing about its greatness and glory, matters with which his readers were conversant; and nothing about its merriment which he apparently failed to observe; but a great deal about the one aspect which won his heart — its very convenient spaciousness. The nations of the world were not then their brothers' keepers, and it took them a long time to find out what their brothers were about:

> Large-hearted age of cakes and ale!
>   When, undeterred by nice conditions,
> Good master Drake would lightly sail
>   On little privateer commissions;
> Careening round with sword and flame,
>   And no pretence of polished manners,
> He Planted out in England's name
>   A most refreshing lot of banners.
>
> No Ministry would care a rap
>   For theoretic arbitration;
> They simply modified the map
>   To meet the latest annexation;
> And so without appeal to law,
>   Or other needless waste of tissue,
> The lion where he put his paw,
>   Remained and propagated issue.

Credit where credit is due. England sent her roving sons over a world in which she was to build a mighty empire. She had the qualities that befit a pioneer. 'The nature of our nation is free, stout, haughty, prodigal of life and blood,' wrote Sir Thomas Smith in 1621. She had also qualities of discretion — reasonableness of outlook, a wise concession to things as they are, and an unfailing grasp on the feasibility of performance. 'The leadership of the world,' says Edward Martin, who evidently believes in such a thing, 'will go to, or remain with, the country that produces the best thinkers and the highest courage.' The leadership of the world would be a sorry task, considering what there is to be led; but steadiness of purpose, coupled with moderation of aim, keeps civilized men from reeling off the track. Elizabeth's England, steady and moderate, was stirred with high hopes and ambitions; but she was short of laughter, and was beginning to want to laugh. That is why clowns overdid their parts, greatly to Hamlet's — or Shakespeare's — annoyance. What the thirteenth century had striven to subdue, the sixteenth century strove robustly to encourage. The pursuit of silenced laughter had begun.

III

THE MERRY MONARCH

A merry monarch, scandalous and poor.
                    EARL OF ROCHESTER

III

THE MERRY MONARCH

THAT was the courtier's point of view, and it became as firmly fixed in men's minds as was the 'merrie England' of Elizabeth. The casual reader has regarded Charles the Second as a witty libertine. The casual critic — with some vague recollections of Macaulay — as a blot on Britain's scutcheon. John Leech, wishing to draw a comprehensive portrait, conceived of him as a satyr, goat-legged and very drunk. That his face was singularly sad, that his mind was singularly acute, are circumstances which have not been suffered to interfere with popular opinion. Yet features are an index to character; and intelligence, while essential to an understanding of the comic spirit, does not lend itself to goatish revelry.

The keynote of the Restoration was a pursuit of pleasure. Not a glad acceptance of pleasure as part of life's experience, but a furious pursuit calculated to defeat its own ends. Just as the unrealities of pacifism — peace congresses, and prizes, and processions, and bands of bewildered young men who solemnly pledge themselves never to bear arms for their country — just as these things are the natural reaction from four years of war, so the unhealthy absorption in pleasure which characterized the Restoration was the natural reaction from eleven years of Puritan rule.

England had never liked this rule. She knew that she was respected abroad, but she also knew that she was uncomfortable at home. She hated the efficiency of military despotism, preferring her inefficient Parliaments which represented constitutional liberty. She hated a life of enforced dulness, wishing to be dull in her own way and at her own discretion. She hated the suppression of holidays and the heavier taxation. John Evelyn said his estate in Essex was so eaten up by taxes that he could not hold on to it. She was depressed by the increase of poverty. The bitter jest of the day was that men no longer gave to beggars because the farthing had disappeared from the currency, and a farthing represented the widest range of almsgiving. Cromwell was strong enough to maintain his government against all discontent and all opposition; but he knew that he had not founded it on the acceptance of the nation, and that it had taken no root.

In London the discontent was deepened by trivial annoyances. Her citizens who had ridden or driven in Hyde Park all their lives resented a tax of sixpence on the horse if they rode, or a shilling on the coach if they drove. It was bad enough to have their theatres, and often their churches, closed; but when it came to their park, they were ripe for the Restoration. The overpowering delight with which that *coup d'état* was received may be measured by the fact that the prayer of thanksgiving which was ordered to be said in the London churches every twenty-ninth of May (the day Charles entered his capital) continued to be recited until 1849. England had in the meantime ridded herself of the Stewarts, worried along under the Hanoverians, and was twelve years deep in Victoria's glorious reign before she stopped thanking God that Charles the Second had come into his own.

'Had this king but loved business as well as he understood it,' said that loyal gentleman, Sir Richard Bulstrode, 'he would have been the greatest prince in Europe.' He would, in fact, have been one of the greatest rulers that England ever had. None more intelligent had filled her throne. But what a fight must have ensued, what a struggle against forces ranged solidly against him — Parliament, Puritanism, bigotry, distrust and credulity walking hand in hand, and the sour withholding of supplies. Even for the fleet, his one kingly pride and joy, Charles could win no support. Disillusioned with monarchy, he surrendered its obligations one by one in favour of its indulgences, and found them an unsatisfactory substitute. For the blood of princes ran in his veins, and the love of England burned in his heart. All of England's kings, good or bad, loved her until she brought over the bored and indifferent Hanoverians. How could the son of Charles the First, and the great-great-grandson of James the Fifth — tragic rulers of England and Scotland — have ever been indifferent?

It is the story of lost leadership. Charles the Second, disappointed in every noble design, thwarted in every rational ambition, turned deliberately to the things he could command. 'So far as it goes,' he said, 'I am the King.' He delighted in wit, and was besotted over women. He knew the worst of both; of wit that was profane and indecent, of women who were gross and greedy. The brief entries in Evelyn's diary are comprehensive and instructive. 'A lewd play,' is his summary of Wycherley's *Country Wife*. 'A very profane wit,' is all he has to say about Rochester. 'This day se'nnight I saw the king sitting and toying with his concubines,' epitomizes his gentlemanly distaste for open immorality. Perhaps it is only fair to state that when these last condemnatory lines were written, all three of the concubines had reached middle age, and that one of them, the mother of grown sons and daughters, had long past the toying and amatory stage. Another, the Duchess of Portsmouth, divined the wishes of the dying king, and had the courage to persuade Barrillon to prompt the Duke of York to bring Father Huddleston into the royal chamber.

'We know the degree of refinement in men,' says George Meredith, 'by the matter they laugh at and by the ring of the laugh.' But a society bent on restoring laughter to a grim world loses nicety and balance. The Commonwealth had made short work of the theatres. An edict of 1649 called for their complete demolition. There was no finical discrimination between the most accomplished tragedian on the boards and the strolling mummer of the countryside. All were classed together as 'rogues according to the law,' and all disappeared — if they were wise — from the eyes of a hostile government. The Restoration opened the theatres wide, freed them from the taxation which the humblest home had to bear, and crowded them in a noisy disorderly fashion. It was at this period that the sober middle-class of London, which had heartily supported the Elizabethan playhouse, withdrew from all participation in an amusement which grew more licentious every year. Sir Richard Garnett says that decent women did go to see the tragedies, but eschewed the comedies, or, if they went, wore masks. As the London harlots also went masked, this compromise was not remarkably protective.

Charles loved the theatre. He was wont to protest against
the custom of making all the villains as black-visaged as he
was himself, but this represented a personal grievance.
Nature and education had fitted him to enjoy the comedy
of manners which reached its zenith with Congreve under
the chilling eye of William the Third. Burnet, paying tribute
to his critical qualities, says that while he had no great
acquaintance with literature, he had, thanks to his training
in France, a correct taste in style, liking what was 'clear,
plain, and short,' and preferring lucidity to all other merits.
If, as we are bidden to believe, the Restoration saw the
birth of modern English prose, and Dryden was its noble
sponsor, the King had a good deal to do with its safe delivery. It took, under his approving eye, the form that
pleased him best. Wit and taste he possessed in a supreme
degree; the deeper emotions he banished as mutinous and
trouble-making; and from poetic vision he was free. That
belonged to the Elizabethan world.

We know that Lamb and Hazlitt, living in an age of
complacent virtue and pretentious mediocrity, were wont
to sigh over the lost drama of the Restoration, and over the
lost libertinism which made such drama acceptable. Perhaps an evening spent with *The Inflexible Captive* or *The
Fatal Falsehood* was calculated to provoke such a sentiment.
'Happy thoughtless age,' sighed Hazlitt, 'when king and
nobles led purely ornamental lives; when the utmost stretch
of a morning's study went no farther than the choice of a
sword-knot, or the adjustment of a side curl; when the soul
spoke out in all the pleasing eloquence of dress.'

As stout a misconception, as misplaced an envy, as ever
were recorded on paper. Charles the Second kept his

throne (that much he had resolved upon from the beginning), and he kept his hold upon the hearts of his people, a circumstance which he found mightily consoling. But what other king of England began his reign with precisely eleven pounds two shillings and tenpence in the national exchequer, to say nothing of a debt of two million pounds bequeathed by the Commonwealth to its successor? What other king of England was called on to face a disastrous war, a disastrous fire, a disastrous plague, a disastrous mock conspiracy, and a disastrous miscarriage of justice which he was powerless to prevent? What other king of England had to defend his wedded wife against the assaults of an English Parliament? What other king of England watched through a goldsmith's window a hostile mob sweep through the streets, insulting his servants and himself? Well might Lord Halifax swear that a wasp's nest was a quieter place to sleep in than London town when Lord Shaftesbury and Titus Oates were sharing its control.

From the violence of factions, from the persecutions of Parliament, from the Act of Uniformity (enough to sour any reign in Christendom), from the inconvenient poverty of a king (rich on paper and poor in coin), and from the defeat of his dearest hopes, Charles turned for refuge to the pleasures which earned for him the epithet 'merry.' He loved good music and good pictures; but he did not love very good books. He loved, like a true Englishman, horse-racing and all outdoor sports. He loved, as though he had been a true Frenchman, good talk and good plays; not the best of plays (Paris heard *Le Misanthrope* and London *The Plain Dealer*), but comedies like *Marriage à la Mode* and tragedies like *Venice Preserved*. He delighted in the satire of

Hudibras, which was but natural. He knew that Butler's assumption that all Puritans were knaves fell short of proof; as a matter of fact Marvell was the man he most admired in England; but he also knew from experience that all Puritans were liable to cant. Their power of disapproval, a power from which they drew strange sustenance and delight, was simply miraculous to a man who found so little in life that called for reprobation.

If Charles loved gay and brilliant talk, he gave more generously than he received. He had no peer for keenness or for charm. He was ever and always the most agreeable of companions. The grace of his manner, the beauty of his voice, made his simplest civilities enchanting to their recipients. They said with conviction that he was 'so pleasant a monarch that no one could be sorrowful in his reign.' He could let pass with a jest the liberty taken by an intoxicated civilian: 'He that is drunk is as good as a king.' He could sit content by the side of a lady mayoress, 'all over scarlet and ermine, and half over diamonds.' He could mingle by day with the crowds at Newmarket, and go at night to see plays acted in a barn by very ordinary Bartholomew Fair comedians. Lord Elgin bears witness to the fact that once on board his yacht, he was 'all mirth and of a most pleasing conversation.' There was in his day great simplicity of essence beneath complexity of manner, and no man was better fitted than Charles for a diffused life of genial enjoyment. His hours of escape heartened him for the hours when he sat grim and silent through the trials of Shaftesbury's victims, or watched Monmouth, his beloved and deeply disloyal son, swaggering in the House of Lords, as though sure of his succession to the throne.

A life of genial enjoyment which means acceptance is vastly different from a life of irrational diversion which means pursuit. The Elizabethans, conscious that laughter was escaping them, encouraged it to stay. The wits of the Restoration, indignant that they had been robbed of laughter for a matter of ten years, set it above price and above codes. 'The comedy of manners,' says George Meredith, 'began as a combative performance, under a license to deride the Puritan, and was here and there Bacchanalian beyond the Aristophanic example; worse, inasmuch as a cynical licentiousness is more abominable than frank filth. The men and women who sat through the acting of Wycherley's *Country Wife* were past blushing.' This degradation of the spirit of comedy inevitably affected the whole field of literature, and stood responsible for the stupidities as well as for the grossness of social life.

There is no shadow of doubt that the rakish society of the Restoration began by tolerating indecency for the sake of wit, and ended by tolerating dulness for the sake of indecency. By 1661 women were playing female parts on the London stage. They were held to be, and frequently were, no better than prostitutes. Twenty years later, English audiences were entertained by hearing girl-children recite epilogues and dialogues full of filthy obscenities. There was nothing amusing about these performances except the suggestion they conveyed of precocious corruption.

'Tis now no Jest to hear young girls talk Bawdy!

voiced in 1682 the weary protest of one Londoner who failed to be diverted. Yet the custom lasted. Charles had been dead ten years and William graced the throne when a six-year-old child, Denny Chock, delighted the play-going world by lisping indecent prologues, which, coming from her infant lips, provoked shouts of laughter. The time was ripe for Jeremy Collier's great protest; and the immediate success of his 'Short View of the Immorality and Profaneness of the Stage' (a work hated with a fury of hatred by Hazlitt) showed plainly enough that existing conditions were tolerated rather than enjoyed.

For the laxness which had demolished decency had also broken down the barriers of taste. The Elizabethans had done without scenery. They were told that they were in Venice, or Denmark, in a Syracusan mart, or on a plain in Syria, and that sufficed them. But a Restoration tragedy was liable to degenerate into a thing of horror or a thing of absurdity because of its setting. Settle's *Empress of Morocco* had a dungeon scene filled with mutilated bodies impaled on stakes; and in *The Siege of Constantinople* the stage direction shows 'a number of men dead or dying in several manners of deaths.' The noise and disorder in the theatre were so great that only an exceptional actor like Betterton could command a hearing. Pepys bears witness to the fact that a fashionable audience preferred talking to listening, and that, as a consequence, he was unable to hear what was said upon the stage. No wonder that *A Midsummer Night's Dream* seemed a tiresome play, and *Othello* a typically bad one, to the careless courtiers who never heard the magic of the lines.

Charles was wittier than the wittiest of his subjects. In this regard the child was father to the man. Many stories are told of his infancy, but one gives perfect promise of the future. He was nine years old when he was confided to the care of William Cavendish, Earl of Newcastle, and his first revolt against authority took the form of refusing physic when he was ill. The Earl appealed to the Queen, who promptly enforced obedience. A month later Newcastle went down with a fever, and his little charge wrote him an affectionate letter, laden with a line of counsel: 'My Lord, I would not have you take too much physic, for it doth always make me worse, and I think it will do the like by you.'

'*La malignité naturelle aux hommes est le principe de la comédie.*' It dictated the letter of the nine-year-old boy, and it prompted the King's flawless jest anent William Penn and his hat; a jest supremely good-tempered which none the less mocked the absurdity of a purely formal pietism.

It was natural that Charles should delight in an accomplishment of which he was a perfect exponent, the interchange of humorous and agreeable civilities. In him, said Chesterton, may be sought and found 'the magnanimous politeness, the dramatic delicacy, which lie on the dim borderland between morality and art.' His friends understood this perfect tone, and strove to imitate it. As a consequence they were liable to rise at times above the level of wit and rottenness which was their habitual *métier*. Even Buckingham,

> A man so various that he seemed to be
> Not one, but all mankind's epitome,

had his occasional flight. Even Sir Charles Sedley, who managed — Heaven knows how! — to produce a play so indecent that it was forbidden the boards, made what amends he could by writing 'Phillis is my only Joy,' a song which has given wise and innocent delight to thousands.

66

Even Rochester, utterly bad and ignoble, was not only a poet and a wit but a loyal husband (constant if not faithful) to the bride he had rudely snatched, and to whom he wrote his best poem. His jests were the bywords of the court. When he said, 'All men would be cowards if they durst,' he merely put into a few words a truism which had hitherto been more expansively voiced; but when he said to a dog which had bitten him, 'I wish you were married and living in the country!' he appealed through a laugh to the suffering heart of humanity. Charles Lamb would have loved that bitter word, and so would Alfred de Musset; the first because he detested the country, the second because he detested both the country and dogs.

Wit was the order of the day. Addison observed of Cowley that his only fault — a pardonable one — was 'wit in excess.' No man won praise which was more worth the winning than did this poet of the Restoration. Dryden said of him, 'His authority is sacred to me,' and Charles said, 'He has left no better man behind him'; flawless epithets both of them, and suited to the reign in which they were spoken. Hazlitt declared that Cowley's 'Anacreontiques' brim over with the spirit of wine and joy. 'Though lengthened out beyond the originals, it is by fresh impulses of an eager and inexhaustible delight.' Yet this exponent of joy describes himself as 'the melancholy Cowley'; and he uttered his full complement of complaints against a world that had treated him well, but in which he observed too often the sharpness of injustice which disturbs men's minds.

We do not turn for wit and humour to Bunyan; but they are qualities which, in common with his age, he possessed.

When he wrote, he said things as neat as this: 'Oaths and obligations in the affairs of the world are like ribbons and knots in dressing. They seem to tie something but do not.' When he spoke, his words were swift and illuminating. 'Ah, Mr. Bunyan, that was a sweet sermon,' said an edified parishioner. 'You need not tell me that,' was the reply. 'The devil whispered it in my ear before I was well out of the pulpit.'

But Bunyan was far from being a merry man. He taught too stern a creed, and he was too prone to apply its precepts to his own harmless life. And the merriment of king and court was a mask, a thing of purpose, a weapon with which to smite the Puritan and take pleasure by storm. 'Genuine humour and true wit,' says Landor, 'require a sound and capacious mind, which is always a grave one.' The gallants of the Restoration who went for amusement to see the chained maniacs of Bedlam, and the women prisoners flogged at Bridewell, and a stallion baited by dogs, were on as wrong a track as any generation that trod before or after them. The poor laws of Charles's reign, as pitiless as those of the Commonwealth, sent foundling children of seven to work in the mines, dragging loads of coal until they dropped dead in their tracks. There was a lack of imagination as well as a lack of feeling when such things were possible; yet now and then, as in the days of Elizabeth, we come suddenly upon the divineness of pity. When Nell Gwynn, the 'unasking' harlot who never was rich, left the sum of twenty pounds a year for the release of some poor debtor or debtors on Christmas Day, she linked her charity to man with the noblest traditions of the Church.

Congreve was but fifteen years of age when Charles the

Second died. In the following fifteen years he wrote his three famous plays, and abandoned the rôle of dramatist. Supremely fortunate in life and death, the friend of great men, the holder of rich sinecures, he sleeps under a fitting monument in Westminster Abbey, and has been extolled as the wittiest of English playwrights. Hazlitt, who sedulously cherished the unrealities of the stage, dreamed of his day as the sons of Adam might have dreamed of Paradise. He thought and said that Congreve's Millamant was better fitted for comedy than was Shakespeare's Rosalind because she was 'more artificial, more theatrical, more meretricious.' Lamb voiced a similar conviction with the courage of one who never sought concurrence. 'That hag, Duty,' having ruled him all his life, his natural reactions were in favour of irresponsibility. He gave his adherence once for all to the form of drama which excludes a moral sense. 'The great art of Congreve is especially shown in this, that he has entirely banished from his scenes — some little generosities of Angelica perhaps excepted — any pretensions to goodness or good feeling whatsoever. Whether he did this designedly or instinctively, the effect is as happy as the design (if design) is bold.'

The effect *is* happy when produced with skill. 'Treasures of sparkling laughter are as wells in our desert,' admits George Meredith. But it is open to one objection. It does not represent life. We can no more imagine a world without goodness or good feeling than we can imagine a world which is all goodness and good feeling. The comedies of the Restoration made no attempt to reflect the manners and morals of the English people, as they were reflected fifty years later in 'Tom Jones'; but only the manners and morals of a small section of the English people, to which, let us hope, they were unjust. Apart from the songs occasionally introduced, they depended upon Dryden for poetic value. Sir Richard Garnett has pointed out that the Elizabethan drama is steeped in poetry. Consequently it will always be read even if it is not acted, and will always be a living force in English literature. The Restoration drama, though it has been occasionally revived (with careful chiselling), is a thing indefinably remote. It deals with types rather than with nature or nationality, and Bunyan was the only man in England who could breathe the breath of life into his types.

Yet hardly had this brilliant and brittle thing passed into the twilight of neglect, when we find the nineteenth century loudly lamenting its loss. It is inevitable that every generation should regret the silenced laughter of its predecessor, and that the echo of these lamentations should come down to us today. Mr. Allardyce Nicoll, who has written a severely critical study of the Restoration drama, forgets his censures when faced with this sense of deprivation. 'Cibber and Farquhar and Vanbrugh,' he says, 'each in his own way, kept the spirit of humour alive for a time, as did later Fielding and Moore and Sheridan and Goldsmith. But the free expression of pure laughter, untouched by thought or by conscience, has passed away for ever.'

So speaks the modern world; but Charles was still on his throne, and England was still rejoicing over the fact, when Dryden penned these lines:

> Then our age was in its prime,
> Free from rage and free from crime,
> A very merry, dancing, drinking,
> Laughing, quaffing and unthinking time.

It sounds — the two last lines certainly sound — like a perfect picture of the Restoration. But the fact is that Dryden placed his blissful period in classic days; and Diana (who must have lived abstemiously to be such a good markswoman) is the divinity in whose praise the jovial chorus is sung. It sweeps us into acquiescence, as a good chorus should always do; and then the poet, clear-eyed and disillusioned, rejects our sympathy, and rejects the claims of the pagan world to permanent delight:

> All, all of a piece throughout;
> The chase had a beast in view;
> The wars brought nothing about;
> The lovers were all untrue;
> 'Tis well an old age is out,
> And time to begin a new.

IV

'HUM'ROUS HOGART'

How singular has been the history of the decline of humour. Is there any profound psychological truth to be gathered from consideration of the fact that it has gone out with cruelty? A hundred years ago — nay fifty years ago — we were a cruel but also a humorous people. We had bull-baitings, and badger-drawings, and hustings, and prize-fights, and cock-fights; we went to see men hanged. With all this we had a broad-blown comic sense. We had Hogarth, and Bunbury, and George Cruikshank, and Gillray. We had the Shepherd of the 'Noctes', and we had Dickens.

ANDREW LANG

IV

'HUM'ROUS HOGART'

THIS is only a renewal of a timeworn complaint. The interesting thing to note is that the list of 'broad-blown' humourists is headed by Hogarth — Hogarth, who preached as consistently as did Bunyan, and whose sermons — as sound as Bunyan's — were, we are asked to believe, regarded by his own generation as comic. Mr. Edmund Blunden tells us authoritatively that Charles Lamb wrote the first study of this great painter in which his genius was analyzed as being 'far above mere burlesque'; and that in so doing the writer was well aware that his point of view was unpopular, inasmuch as England preferred the joke to the sermon. Lamb's attitude was firmly fixed when, as a child, he gazed day after day upon the prints of 'The Rake's Progress' and 'The Harlot's Progress' which hung on the walls of Blakesware. Children are impervious to satire, and these pictures are not satiric. They tell their story with violence, but violence restrained within the limits of accuracy. 'Other prints we look at,' said Lamb, 'these we read'; and few adults can peruse paint-brush fiction with the deep attention, the lasting memory, of a child. Compare Hazlitt 'bursting his sides' over an artist 'whose pictures are a jest-book from one end to the other' with Lamb's seriousness, and his prim commentary in a letter to Thomas Manning: 'In my best room is a choice collection of the works of Hogarth, an English painter of some humour.'

'Some humour' has a chilling sound; but Lamb's delight in the chimney-sweeper who stands grinning in the 'March to Finchley' is a tribute to mirth 'snatched out of desolation.' Sweeps were dear to Hogarth as to Lamb because they were part and parcel of 'London with-the-many-sins.' Hogarth painted the London streets as other artists painted hills and meadows; and that 'prodigious abundance of human knowledge,' which is our wonder and delight, was the gift of the great city to her favourite son. Lamb loved these crowded canvases with not a 'furniture face' in the crowd. He loved the littered rooms. Not a cat or a kitten, not a broken pipe or a picture on the wall escaped his close attention. If he wondered a little why so many depraved characters were noseless, he granted to the delineator the right to deal with features as he felt inclined.

It was a strong-stomached generation. Nothing was coarse enough to sicken it. It was an outspoken generation which called things by their biblical names. Hogarth had the good fortune to belong to his own time as distinctively as he belonged to his own race and to his own birthplace. 'He was a moralist after the fashion of eighteenth-century morality,' says Mr. Austin Dobson; 'not savage like Swift, nor ironical like Fielding, nor tender like Goldsmith; but unrelenting, uncompromising, uncompassionate; peopling his canvas with vivid types of that cynical and sensual, brave and boastful, corrupt and patriotic age.'

What is perfectly plain to Mr. Dobson is Hogarth's careful exclusion of humour from scenes where it might have softened the moral he meant to convey. The 'Election Prints' are triumphantly comic. They deal with a subject which has provoked laughter for generations, and which, in our own time, George Birmingham has made as absurd and as diverting as ever. There is no subtlety in Hogarth's treatment of this familiar theme. He did not know the meaning of the word. His 'Canvassing for Votes' has the simple candour of 'Pickwick.' It was a great help to the painter to know that a vote could be bought like any other piece of merchandise in the open market, and that nobody paid more than it was worth. Our modern system of polling presents no such compensatory features.

Hogarth *was* uncompassionate. So presumably was Rhadamanthus, and there is something Rhadamantine in Hogarth's administration of justice. Thackeray in an unregenerate moment confessed to a sentiment of pity for Tom Idle, the apprentice whose name damned him from the start. He said he was glad that the Toms of his day had a better chance than when Hogarth painted and Fielding hanged them. But then Thackeray also confessed to a downright affection for the Artful Dodger and Charley Bates, an affection which Dickens (who did not hesitate to make his young thieves amusing) would have condoned, but which Hogarth would have thought indefensible. 'Industry and Idleness' is a sermon undisguised, with every circumstance fitted neatly into place, which is the privilege of the preacher. But to one who has known it from early childhood, as Lamb knew his 'Harlot' and his 'Rake,' and has believed in it with the credulity of innocence, the prints are charming, especially the one in which the correct young couple are singing out of the same hymn book in church. And the antiquarian can-

not fail to be pleased when the industrious apprentice mar-
ries his master's daughter, and the butchers in the street play
manfully on the 'hymenaean,' that combination of marrow-
bone and cleaver which when properly struck produced, so
we are assured, 'no despicable clang.'

This is cheerful if not laughable. Hogarth had then no
more thought of diverting his public than had Solomon
when he said, 'Go to the ant, thou sluggard.' No more than
when he painted 'Gin Lane' and 'Beer Street' to show that
destitution and disease followed the drinking of imported
Hollands (which entered England with William the Third),
and that health and prosperity blessed all good topers who
drank home-brewed beer:

> — warming each English generous heart
> With liberty and love.

It was, as Mr. Dobson has noted, a patriotic age, and
Hogarth was nothing if not a patriot. Foreigners to him
meant Frenchmen (he had been to France and did not like
it), and the most despicable thing about them was their lean-
ness. Pampered priests might be swollen with food, but the
rest of the people were starvelings. The curious notion that
the nation, as a nation, lived on frogs was prevalent, and
was considered comical. Even Garrick, who knew better,
made merry over the idea that such a diet could nourish
soldiers:

> Beef and beer give heavier blows
> Than soup and toasted frogs.

A century later the same thought found expression in an
Ingoldsby Legend which pictured 'a cold sirloin big enough
to frighten a Frenchman.'

Hogarth's antipathy to France was more than a distaste. It was a sound, all-embracing disapproval which included every circumstance of life. 'Poverty, slavery, and innate insolence covered with an affectation of politeness, give you a true picture of the manners of the whole nation,' he wrote with that pleasing self-assurance which the civilized man occasionally shares with the savage.

Holland was less iniquitous (being unvisited) than France; but its intoxicant was so deadly that it made the very houses in Gin Lane totter to their fall. Lamb, who compared this terrible picture to Poussin's 'Plague at Athens,' gave it precedence as being more imaginative and more replete with strange images of death. 'Every thing contributes to bewilder and stupefy. The houses tumbling about in various directions seem drunk' — whereas the Athenian dwellings remain untouched by disease. It certainly did not occur to this sympathetic critic to see anything humorous in the scene, or he would not have made his comparison (no one is expected to laugh at the plague); but he is the only commentator who does not draw our attention to the fact that the single evidence of prosperity in Gin Lane is given by the pawnbroker's shop, whereas the same business in Beer Street languishes for lack of custom. Times had changed since the days of Skelton when a workman's wife would pawn her husband's cap and hood

Because the ale is good.

Hogarth's enmity toward all things foreign extended itself to those Continental artists who were popularly spoken of as the 'old masters.' Rembrandt was his particular detestation (he had never seen the 'Night Watch'), and Correggio ran a close second. Having painted his 'Sigismonda' to show that he could 'rival the ancients on their own ground,' he refused to sell the picture for less than four hundred pounds, that being the sum for which a presumed Correggio (really a Furini) had been recently bought in London. Possible purchasers being unable to see the compelling force of this argument, 'Sigismonda' remained unsold; and the painter, nailing his colours to the mast, forbade his wife, or widow, to part with it for less than the original price. After her death it was bought by the Boydells for fifty-six guineas, and now hangs in the National Gallery. The best thing that critics have found to say about it is that it is in excellent preservation.

Hogarth's portraits had better fortune, the most immediately successful being that of Garrick as Richard III, for which, as he proudly tells us, he was paid two hundred pounds; 'more than any English artist ever received for a portrait, and that too by the sanction of several painters who had previously been consulted about the price, which was not given without mature consideration.' Garrick was a difficult subject to paint because, though he could assume at will any expression he chose, he could not, or did not, keep that expression long. The Richard III look passed into something less tense while Hogarth was striving to convey it to the canvas. On the other hand, it is said that the actor was of help to the artist when the latter was endeavouring to paint a portrait of the dead Fielding. Garrick did not in the least resemble Fielding; but he could mould his features into something which was like a resemblance because it conveyed characteristics. The gay little sketch of Mrs. Garrick taking the pen from her husband's hands passed eventually into the possession of George the Fourth, who, unlike his predecessors, knew a good thing when he saw it.

The friendship between Hogarth and Garrick was firm and lasting. 'He is a great and original Genius,' wrote the player to Churchill. 'I love him as a Man and reverence him as an Artist. I would not for all the Politicks and Politicians in the universe that you two should have the least cause of ill-will toward each other.' In his prologue to *The Clandestine Marriage* he gave spirited praise to 'matchless Hogarth,' to the artist 'who pictured Morals and Mankind, and whose object in so doing was to make mankind more moral.' On that point, at least, there was never any doubt.

Walpole, who considered that 'as a painter Hogarth had but slender merit,' patronized him timidly, and invited him to dine with the poet Gray — a not very successful dinner. Host and guest had but little in common save an intense aversion to cruelty, especially cruelty to animals, in which regard they were, as Mr. Lang avers, far in advance of their time. Yet Walpole said one word — and said it with his customary precision — that would have given more pleasure to Hogarth than all the praise that has ever been lavished upon him: 'He observes the true end of comedy — reformation.'

Dr. Johnson and Hogarth first met at the home of Richardson. Hogarth, a warm Hanoverian, was expressing his amazement that George the Second, whom he considered a clement man, should have refused a pardon to Dr. Cameron — as guiltless a rebel as ever graced a scaffold. Johnson, who had been standing somewhat apart looking out of a window, came forward suddenly and burst into a torrent of words, accusing the King of harshness and heartlessness. Hogarth, unacquainted with the speaker, was petrified with wonderment at his manner, which was agitated to the verge of violence, and at his arguments, which were persuasive and convincing. He reached the justifiable conclusion that the stranger was certainly mad, and that his madness was certainly inspired.

The two men were eminently fitted to appreciate each other's merits. Hogarth said to Boswell that Johnson's conversation was as far above the talk of other men as Titian's portraits were above those of Thomas Hudson; a comparison which proves that there was at least one old master whose greatness the British painter reverently admitted. Dr. Johnson's emendation of Garrick's epitaph on Hogarth is certainly an improvement on the original. The two lines,

> Here Death has closed the curious eyes
> That saw the manners in the face,

show what can be done with a simple phrase, 'the curious eyes,' when it chances to be the right one.

The jovial parson who is ladling out punch in the 'Modern Midnight Conversation' was a relative of Dr. Johnson's, a gentleman named Ford. As the print hung on the walls of the dining-room at Streatham, the doctor had every opportunity of identifying his kinsman. He does not seem to have taken umbrage at the discredit done the cloth, being the most lenient as well as the staunchest of churchmen; ready to forgive a laggard for not attending the service on Sunday, provided he doffed his hat when he passed the sacred edifice on week-days. His comment on Ford was brief and calm: 'I have been told he was a man of good parts; profligate but not impious.'

Among the points of resemblance between Hogarth and

Dr. Johnson may be reckoned a strong distaste for Papists and dissenters. Methodists appear to have affected Hogarth as Puritans affected 'Hudibras.' The confused medley entitled 'Credulity, Superstition, and Fanaticism' is supposed to be directed against Methodism, though no member of that church, nor of any other, would ever know it. It is true that Whitefield's 'Journal' is placed prominently on a hassock under the reading-desk, a hassock which in the first impression was occupied by a dog wearing a collar inscribed G. Whitefield. But as that far-travelled preacher was as much of a Calvinist as a Methodist, and as all forms of religion outside the English Establishment are impartially insulted in both prints, honours are easy. Hogarth painting allegory is as lost as Fielding would have been writing a symbolic Maeterlinckian drama. His passion for detail traps him into strewing his canvas with an assortment of mysterious odds and ends, every one of which means something that it isn't.

The respect accorded to such work as 'Credulity, Superstition, and Fanaticism,' and the obscure 'Bathos,' was due to the firmly established belief that, as Hogarth was primarily a moralist, every picture preached. Walpole, indeed, observed that 'for useful and deep satire the print on the Methodist is the most sublime'; but Walpole's dislike for this particular brand of dissenters was as strong as Hogarth's, or as Dr. Johnson's, or as Sydney Smith's. Anything that could be construed into an attack upon them would have seemed to him sublime. 'The Bathos' was designed as a travesty on the unforgiven 'old masters'; but it would have answered just as well as a satire on ambition, or covetousness, on war, or peace, on ignorance, or learning. The main thing was to make sure of a moral which, like the 'Application' of Aesop's Fables, took up much time and attention. If there was a slackening on the painter's part, he was promptly reminded of his duty. One admirer wrote to warn him that he had rivals in art, but that no one had ever attempted to equal him in the moral walk. Another besought him, as a moralist, to protest against the cruelty and cupidity of the cockpit, which he did after a fashion so lusty that his contemporaries may not have recognized the very popular print as a remonstrance.

It is hard to believe with Mr. Blunden that Charles Lamb was the first writer to raise the genius of Hogarth 'far above mere burlesque,' when we read the kind of things which were written during the painter's lifetime and immediately after his death. His prints were used as texts for sermons, and were commented upon with that sincere regard for the obvious which is the most popular characteristic of the pulpit. A volume entitled 'Hogarth Moralized' was published in 1768 by John Trusler, a gentleman who did not hesitate to paint the lily, and whose kindly purpose it was to assist people to see what they could not possibly miss. Thus the 'Harlot's Progress' teaches us that 'a deviation from virtue is a departure from happiness'; and 'Marriage à la Mode' enables us to 'form a just estimate of the value of riches and high life when abused by prodigality or degraded by vice.' Commenting on 'Industry and Idleness,' Mr. Trusler calls our attention to the happy crowds that turn out to see the industrious apprentice made Lord Mayor of London, and to the no less happy crowds that turn out to see the idle apprentice hanged, and observes with sprightly intelligence: 'After this it would be unnecessary to say which is the more

eligible path to tread.' Even the portrait of Garrick as
Richard III, which, being but a portrait, would seem innocent of texts, conveys its lesson to the world. Mr. Trusler
goes back of Hogarth, back of Shakespeare, and landing
safely in history, 1485, is able to authoritatively inform us
that 'naught is productive of solid happiness but inward
peace and serenity of mind.'

And this was the generation which we are bidden to believe regarded Hogarth's prints as a giant jest-book. This
was the England envied by Mr. Lang for its 'broad-blown
comic sense.' This was the artist whom Lamb rescued from
the ranks of 'mere burlesque,' and over whose pictures Hazlitt burst his sides with laughter. Who would venture to say
that Hogarth's mirth is 'heart-easing'? Better than any
man that ever lived he knew how the grotesque elbows the
terrible. The wise child, Charles Lamb, recognized this
alliance. He felt it in the last scene of 'The Rake's Progress,'
where two finely dressed, simpering ladies have come to be
entertained by the tragic absurdities of Bedlam.

'The Four Stages of Cruelty' are as definitely removed
from the field of humour as from the field of art. So Hogarth
meant them to be. He took little pains with the designs, and
did not consider that careful engraving was necessary. He
wanted them to be as cheap as possible so as to be within
the means of the class he hoped to reach. They were intended
for one purpose only, and he said that if they achieved this
purpose he would be more proud of them than if he had
painted Raphael's cartoons; a remark which proves that he
did not undervalue the beauty of the cartoons.

Whether the depraved and vicious were made good and
kind by these dreadful pictures we shall never know; but

people who were already good and kind wrote lengthy hom-
ilies in praise of goodness and kindness. They even dropped
into verse to make their words persuasive, and this verse was
printed as an accompanying text for the illustrations. In the
first and most hideous of the series a little lad pleads for the
tortured dog, an incident which is thus described by the poet:

> Behold! a youth of gentler heart,
>   To spare the creature pain,
> 'O take,' he cries, 'take all my tart!'
>   But tears and tart are vain.

The appeal is pleasantly reminiscent of a still more generous
child in the ballad of the 'Cruel Step-mother':

> Then outspake the scullery lad,
>   In a loud voice spake he:
> 'Oh, spare her life, good master cook,
>   And make your pies of me.'

Horace Walpole was so deeply impressed by the 'Four
Stages of Cruelty' that he read into the fourth (which is
really an anticlimax, being only a dissection room with
nobody cruel in it) a moral which he proclaimed solemnly
to his world: 'How delicate and superior is Hogarth's satire
when he intimates in the College of Physicians and Surgeons
that preside at the dissection, how the legal habitude of
viewing shocking scenes hardens the human mind, and ren-
ders it unfeeling. The president maintains the dignity of
insensibility over an executed corpse, and considers it but
as the object of a lecture.' How else could he have considered it, we naturally ask; but it is only fair to say that Tom
Nero's corpse, being of Walpole's mind, appears to be protesting gruesomely against the liberties taken with it — lib-

erties which are loathsome without a suggestion of purpose. What, one wonders, did the travelled Walpole think of the serene and serious Tulp discoursing to his seven associates in Rembrandt's 'Lesson in Anatomy'? A certain horror emanates from that great canvas, but it is an awe-inspiring horror; it has the dignity of science and the seemliness of art.

There is no shadow of doubt that Hogarth's contemporaries regarded the 'Enraged Musician' as purely comic, and were by way of thinking the 'Distrest Poet' diverting. The musician is plainly a foreigner, and it serves him right to be deafened by the racket of a London street. Today, when noise is one of the recognized evils of the world, our sympathy for the poor fiddler is modified by the thought that he lived and died before the advent of the radio. The din that torments him is, after all, transient. The bawling woman, the pipe-playing Jew, the child with a drum will pass on, they are only human; the radio alone has the infernal permanence of mechanism.

The details of the 'Distrest Poet' are made as absurd as possible to lessen the painfulness of the subject. A poverty-stricken poet is as tragic as a poverty-stricken knife-grinder (Chatterton was a poet); but Hogarth desired the picture to be humorous, which, in a fashion, it is. Possibly he also desired 'A Modern Midnight Conversation' to be as amusing as satire could make it. English critics were disposed to think it a temperance tract of tremendous force and vigour; but in Germany, where the plate was very popular, its moral lesson played a minor rôle. It may be found painted on German porcelain pipes, and engraved on snuff boxes. If the drinker who is vomiting his liquor, and the drinker who tumbles headlong and wigless to the floor, illustrate the tract, the drinker who is trying to light his pipe with a candle, and lights his sleeve instead, is felicitously and flawlessly funny.

Hogarth was himself a man of temperate habits and of cheerful conversation; easily offended, needlessly quarrelsome, and staunchly loyal to his friends. He had the reputation of being parsimonious, for no apparent reason save that he paid his debts, which seems to have been considered a miserly thing to do. He did not believe that the poor were more virtuous than the rich, but he loved fair play. Had he been a sportsman, he would have been best pleased when a wise and wary hare eluded the dogs. He gave the chimney-sweeps whom he sketched in 'Chairing the Member' a half-crown apiece, and he would not permit his servants to take fees from clients who came to have their portraits painted. Like all self-made men, he undervalued the things he did not know. He was more insular than Hannah More, and his 'clamorous rudeness' in France expressed his annoyance that even such an inferior country should be peopled by Frenchmen. His friends loved and honoured him, and told pleasant stories of his candour, simplicity, and absent-mindedness. He went once to visit Beckford, then Lord Mayor of London, driving sedately in his new coach decorated with a highly emblematic crest; and, coming out into the pouring rain, forgot all about the waiting vehicle, and walked home drenched and unconcerned as in his apprentice days.

A coach indicates extravagance, but Hogarth had little chance to be extravagant. His paintings sold badly because of his absurd insistence on auctioning them. The six masterpieces which make up 'Marriage à la Mode' were timidly purchased in 1750 for a hundred and twenty-six pounds. In less than fifty years they were resold for fourteen hundred pounds, and they are now worth any conceivable sum. The admirable and highly comic 'Election' series were bought by the wise Garrick for two hundred guineas, and became the most precious possession of his life. The 'March to Finchley,' a picture of irresistible and irreclaimable disorder, was first dedicated to George the Second, who having, as Walpole expresses it, 'little propensity to refined pleasures,' considered it an insult to his Foot Guards, and expressed such Hanoverian wrath that the dedication was transferred to the King of Prussia, as 'an encourager of Arts and Sciences.' That redoubtable monarch, who tolerated no disorder, but to whom no flattery came amiss, made a handsome acknowledgment of the compliment. The painting was sold by lottery, and Hogarth gave the unpurchased tickets to the Foundling Asylum, which became the owner of this rather incongruous prize. A few years later the artist presented to the same institution his 'Moses Brought to Pharaoh's Daughter,' a perfectly suitable subject, but a bad picture, and therefore no prize at all.

If Hogarth was unfortunate in the sale of his paintings, the prints brought him a steady income. They never lacked subscribers, and some of them, like 'Industry and Idleness,' enjoyed years of unbroken popularity. Always at Christmas time there was a demand for these admonitory pictures, which we have reason to fear were given, like admonitory books, by uncles and godparents to imperfect youth. The most dramatic success was that accorded to the print of Lord Lovat. When this unregenerate rebel was brought from Scotland to London, Hogarth met him at St. Albans, and

made a rapid, masterly sketch of the eighty-year-old Jacobite
for whom the scaffold was waiting. The trial, the execution,
and the grim humour with which the condemned met his
well-merited death, aroused so tense an interest that a London
book-seller actually offered its weight in gold (which sounds
like the prodigal East) for the copper plate on which the
drawing was engraved. The offer was wisely refused. The
prints were in such demand that the rolling presses worked
day and night to supply them. They sold for a shilling each,
and Hogarth made twelve pounds a day as long as the excitement lasted. He had also the pleasant recollection that the
old lord was so glad to see him at St. Albans that he stopped
midway in shaving to kiss his welcome visitor, and transferred
the lather to his cheek.

In all this there is little to suggest the uproarious mirth
which so delighted Hazlitt. The academic 'Pool of Bethesda'
and the 'Good Samaritan' are decorous mural paintings presented by the artist to St. Bartholomew's Hospital. The spirited 'Shrimp Girl' in the National Gallery expresses nothing
but its own comeliness and bloom. The treatise on the
'Analysis of Beauty' amused unfriendly critics when it was
published; but all that is left of it today is a serpentine line
drawn on the palette of Hogarth's best and most familiar
self-portrait — the one with his dog, Trump, and what Leigh
Hunt describes as 'a sort of knowing jockey look.' He was
undoubtedly, as Hazlitt says, 'one of the greatest comic gen-
iuses that ever lived'; but — Mr. Lang to the contrary — it
was not as a humourist that he valued himself and was valued by his contemporaries. He was actuated by a sincere
desire to benefit and improve mankind, to leave the world
better than he found it. 'I have invariably endeavoured to

make those about me tolerably happy,' he wrote with enviable assurance, 'and my greatest enemy cannot say I ever
did an intentional injury; though without ostentation I could
produce many instances of men that have been essentially
benefited by me.'

The rising fame of Sir Joshua Reynolds partially eclipsed
Hogarth's renown. The amazing distinction of Reynolds's
portraits, which seemed to convey to the beholder a revelation of what was essentially distinguished in English character, gave to his art a supreme and noble significance. For
an understanding of his work no one could do better than
read Santayana's 'Soliloquies in England.' But Hogarth's
fame rests on a sure foundation, and he has never lacked the
affectionate regard of artists. Whistler, for example, praised
him in season and out of season; but with Whistler, as with
Lamb, it was a question of sympathetic recollection rather
than of criticism. A little sick boy with a blistered chest
tucked into an arm chair with a great volume of Hogarth's
prints propped securely on the bed, near enough for him to
turn the pages. It is as perfect a setting as that of the child,
Charles Lamb, wandering solitary and content through the
halls of Blakesware. He had only the 'Harlot's Progress' and
the 'Rake's Progress' to delight him, whereas little James
McNeill Whistler had the whole rich array spread out before his ravished eyes. 'From this time until his death,' said
Mrs. Pennell, 'he always believed Hogarth to be the greatest
English artist who ever lived, and he seldom lost an opportunity of saying so.'

The three words 'from this time' give the situation away.
For all of us there are memories which take the place of
judgment. And moreover it was possible that Whistler

hoped some one would disagree with him. Joseph Pennell gave an amusing account of Mr. Harper Pennington, who had been told that Hogarth was a caricaturist, and who thought, not unnaturally, that it had been left for his eyes to discover the artist. He looked long and closely at the superb collection in the National Gallery, and then said with emphasis to the amused Whistler, 'Hogarth was a great painter.' 'Sh — sh! — yes — I know it,' was the answer. 'But don't you tell 'em.'

If Reynolds portrayed the quality of distinction which is an attribute of the few, Hogarth portrayed the recognizable qualities of the many. Better than any artist, and as well as any author that ever lived, he understood and expressed British temperament in the bulk, 'from the battle of Blenheim to the loss of the American colonies.' It was this clear understanding which won for him the admiration of a very great man who likewise knew humanity in the bulk, and served it loyally. The last gratifying episode of Hogarth's life was the receipt of 'an agreeable letter from the American, Dr. Franklin.' The painter was ill when this letter came; but it roused him from the apathy of weakness, and he scribbled a few lines meant to be the rough draft of an answer. Two hours later he was dead.

V

THE STAGE AND THE PULPIT

Sheridan's Comic Muse is garlanded, and crowned with roses and vine leaves. Her eyes sparkle with delight, and her heart runs over with good-natured malice. She shows her laughing face, and points to her rich treasure — the follies of mankind.

WILLIAM HAZLITT

English gaiety is seldom come at lawfully. Friendship, or propriety, or principle is sacrificed to obtain it. We cannot produce it without more effort than it is worth. Our destiny is to look vacant and sit silent.

SYDNEY SMITH

V

THE STAGE AND THE PULPIT

T HERE they stand, side by side, comments worth considering. Reading them, two thoughts penetrate into our puzzled minds. Had Sheridan remained faithful to his muse,
he might have had a merry instead of a tragic old age. Had
Sydney Smith lived up to his own severe dictum, he would
certainly have died a bishop.

Hazlitt was but one year old when the first representa-
tion of *The School for Scandal* crowned Sheridan, not with
roses only, but with unfading laurels. His words of praise
are fraught with that desire to hear lost laughter which is
the burden of every century's lament. He lived in a day of
mediocrity. Lamb said of him that he was the only man in
London whose conversation was worth listening to; and he
might have said the same of Lamb, save that there was Theodore Hook flashing meteor-like through the social world,
and there was Coleridge, who, if listened to long enough,
was sure to say something memorable. Hazlitt, who had a
passion for the stage, never disassociated Sheridan from his
early triumphs, and probably never thought of him save as
portrayed by Byron — as the irresistible talker to whom he
(Byron), Rogers, and Moore had listened from six P.M. until
one, without a yawn among them.

Yet Sheridan could be monumentally dull; witness his epilogue to Voltaire's *Sémiramis*. The play, as adapted by Captain Ayscough, had reduced a good-natured audience to the verge of despair; and before they could escape and forget it, the epilogue caught them, and preached them a sermon which they were in no mood to hear. It assumed that they had been deeply moved by the tragedy, and bade them turn this emotion to good account:

> Thou child of sympathy, whoe'er thou art,
> Who with Assyria's Queen has wept thy part,
> Go, search where keener woes demand relief,
> Go, while thy heart still beats with fancied grief,
> Thy lips still conscious of the recent sigh,
> The graceful tear still lingering in thine eye,
> Go, and on real misery bestow
> The blessed effusion of fictitious woe.

And this untimely discourse, this pretentious elegance (the 'graceful tear' is worthy of the Swan of Litchfield), came from the pen of Sheridan, whose incomparable wit held friends by his side and creditors at bay, who could charm a bailiff and soften the heart of an attorney. 'There has been nothing like it,' said Byron, 'since the days of Orpheus.'

For some unfathomable reason Lord Hertford delayed to license *The School for Scandal* until a few hours before its first performance — a nerve-racking experience for everyone concerned. Its brilliant success ('a marvellous resurrection of the stage,' said Horace Walpole) should have brought contentment even to Sheridan, who never was contented, and who had pronounced its predecessor, *The Rivals*, to be the worst play in the English language — which he knew very well it wasn't. A mysterious story concerning the origin of *The School for Scandal* attracted the attention of that large body of people who are ready to believe that anyone except the author wrote a book, or a play, or a poem. It was whispered that this masterpiece was the work of a nameless young lady in ill health who offered it to Sheridan for production, and who died immediately and conveniently at Bath, thus enabling the manager of Drury Lane to appropriate it as his own.

Why did a dramatist who was the first in his field abandon that field so lightly? Why, having written *The School for Scandal*, *The Critic*, and *The Duenna*, thus easily outdistancing all rivals, did he turn his back upon the Muse, 'crowned with roses and vine leaves,' and take the dusty path of politics? It is true that the management of Drury Lane overwhelmed him with debt, and its destruction by fire in 1809 ruined him. But Sheridan would have been overwhelmed with debt in Utopia, and financially ruined in the Garden of Paradise. It was his appointed fate. Garrick could make the great theatre pay its way, pay its company, and pay himself liberally; but Sheridan could do none of these things. Yet he had abundant energy, and was industrious, his only labour-saving device being to leave his letters unopened. For this no humane man will blame him; but it is an expedient which eventually leads to confusion. Another pardonable weakness was a disregard of time. 'Sheridan's days are weeks,' observed his sister-in-law, Mrs. Tickell, with the inflexible accuracy of relationship.

Byron is largely responsible for the popular view of Sheridan — a man always witty, often drunk, and never possessed of a shilling. On the last point he dwells with all the persistency of error. He says that Sheridan told him once, 'I have never had a shilling of my own' — 'though to be sure,' mused the poet, 'he contrived to extract a good many of other people's.' In 1818 Byron wrote to Moore a letter full of good advice and good feeling: 'Remember that Sheridan never had a shilling, and was thrown, with great powers and passions, into the thick of the world, and placed upon the pinnacle of success, with no external means to support him in his elevation.'

But we know that as manager of Drury Lane he could count for some years on an income of several thousand pounds, and that after the production of *The School for Scandal* and *The Critic*, this income was temporarily increased. His first wife, the incomparable Miss Linley, 'half muse, half angel,' kept the accounts, and probably kept them badly — accounts not coming within the province of either angel or muse. That he had property is proved by the fact that he left it unencumbered to his second wife, and that she lived on it and on her own dowry until she died. It was insufficient to support him when he entered Parliament, and became 'a splendid drudge without permanent pay.' A brilliant and aggressive member of a brilliant and aggressive Opposition is not presumed to be on the road to wealth. He did, however, receive from his patron, the Prince of Wales, the sinecure of the Receivership of the Duchy of Cornwall, which carried a salary of eight hundred pounds. Altogether, he had a number of shillings of his own, and spent them with enjoyment.

Again it seems to have been Byron's ill or good fortune to have found Sheridan in a state of perpetual intoxication. 'He got drunk very thoroughly and very soon.' It was to

Byron that he told the tale of his being locked up by a watchman who encountered him, tipsy and bellicose, in the London streets on the opening night of *The School for Scandal*. It
was Byron who, after a convivial evening, conducted him
carefully down 'a damned corkscrew staircase, built before
the time of spirituous liquors.' It was Byron who disen-
tangled the intricacies of a forgotten engagement with
Rogers, and wrote the best explanation he could to the disappointed host: 'Sheridan was yesterday at first too sober
to remember your invitation; but in the dregs of a third
bottle he fished up his memory, and found that he had a
party at home.'

The friendly relation between dramatist and poet was
never broken. Sheridan told Byron that he cared little for
poetry in general, and not at all for his, a verdict which
Byron received with perfect good temper. He was not exact-
ing on this point. To him we owe a truer knowledge of
Sheridan than any biographers have given us. Byron delighted in his friend's wit, 'always saturnine and sometimes
savage'; insisted that his drunkenness was Bacchic, never
reaching the Selinus stage; cherished an ardent admiration
for his genius, and wrote a sincerely felt, but somewhat thun-
derous, monody on his death.

It was Sheridan's opinion that Byron would have made
a good orator. He founded his view on the denunciations of
'English Bards and Scotch Reviewers,' having apparently
no conception of an oration which should be otherwise than
denunciatory. In the days of Burke and Fox the Opposition
was a magnificent field for invective. George the Third was
enough to drive any sane man into it; but the Prince of
Wales was more than enough to drive any sane man out

99

again. Sheridan boasted that the Prince gave him 'his entire and unqualified confidence.' He said in the House of
Commons: 'The protecting friendship with which his Royal
Highness has condescended to honour me for so many years
has formed the just pride of my life.' The 'entire and unqualified confidence' meant that when the Prince had author-
ized Fox to deny in the House his marriage to Mrs. Fitzher-
bert, and had then frankly admitted it, he selected Sheridan as the man best fitted to straighten things out with the
lady. The 'protecting friendship' meant that, after sum-
moning his friend night after night to Carlton House, to
talk over his affairs until four A.M., 'not supping or with a
drop of wine,' he did not, after Sheridan's death, send so
much as a line of condolence to his widow. It was left for
the Duke of Wellington to come forward with generous sympathy and offers of assistance. That the Prince's all-embracing vanity was not lost on his loyal follower is proven by
Sheridan's careless remark: 'What his Royal Highness particularly prides himself upon is the late excellent harvest.'

Sheridan the legislator lost the sound of laughter which
had echoed through the life of Sheridan the dramatist and
manager, and the world has shared his loss. There was com-
pensation, doubtless, in the thrilled attention with which his
fellow members of Parliament listened to speeches three and
four days long. The wonder to us now is not so much the
continuity of the speaker as the endurance of the audience.
Sheridan, like Gladstone, stood ready to reform the solar
system. Unhappily reformation, which is a profitable line
of business today, was a dead loss in 1788, when Warren
Hastings was impeached on charges of corruption and
cruelty. The eloquence let loose during that remarkable

trial flooded the country, and we hear faint washings of the tide today. Burke's fame rose to its highest pinnacle, Sheridan's was little less brilliant — and Hastings was acquitted. So great was the enthusiasm aroused by Sheridan's first speech in behalf of the begums of Oudh (even the dispassionate Sir Gilbert Elliot pronounced it a masterpiece) that when the following year he addressed the High Court of Parliament, men paid fifty pounds for a seat. What is more remarkable, they blocked the entrance to Westminster Hall at six A.M., although the Court did not sit until noon.

It was a great opportunity, and Sheridan made the most of it. He probably knew that the begums were rich and rapacious old ladies playing a close game; but was there ever an Irishman who could not make a heartbreaking appeal in behalf of defenceless womanhood, and was there ever an Englishman who could remain unmoved by it? In the present instance, the Irishman appealed and the Englishmen listened for three days. On the third, when the impassioned utterances had reached their climax, Sheridan gasped out, 'My Lords, I have done' (words they must have been glad to hear), and sank exhausted into the arms of Burke, who stood waiting to receive him. Only a few fragments of this oratory have been left to us — a circumstance not to be regretted. Burke always said that a speech which read well was a damned bad speech, and what he did not know on the subject was hardly worth the knowing.

The death of Burke and of Fox left the Opposition without leaders. The Prince of Wales, elevated to the Regency, found his former friends to be undesirable acquaintances. Sheridan, sad, infirm, hard pressed by creditors (whose natural desire to be paid has always been harshly criticized), was nevertheless surrounded by care and comfort. A sheriff's officer was domiciled in the house where he lay dying; but three of London's leading physicians came every day to help him die, and the very eminent Bishop Howley came every few days with the same laudable purpose. The sick man had never been indifferent to the pomp and glory of the grave ('There is snug lying in Westminster Abbey,' he said); and thither after death he was borne in more state, and with a much longer procession, than had fallen to the lot of Fox, or even Pitt. It is said that he desired to be buried by the side of Fox, and that the 'Poets' Corner' where he was laid held no attraction for him. But the Muse whom he had flouted in life triumphed in death, and has gone on triumphing ever since. We read about his speeches, but we see — when we can — his plays. If Mrs. Malaprop has grown wearisome, the Absolutes, father and son, still live. If the scandal-mongering of Snake and Lady Sneerwell becomes unbearably monotonous, the auction of the family portraits is good comedy. It illustrates to perfection Hazlitt's analysis of the play, 'which professes a faith in the natural goodness as well as in the habitual depravity of human nature.'

The playgoer laments to this day that Sheridan, aged thirty-one, turned his back upon the stage in favour of Parliament and speech-making; but there is no shadow of doubt that he chose the life he loved. He did not want to walk with silver slippers in the sunshine; he wanted the stress and strain of battle. It may be remembered that Miss Jane Addams, the mouthpiece of American sensibility, said twenty years ago that 'dulness will no longer be a necessary attribute of public life when gracious and grey-haired women become part of it.' It would have been hard for Sheridan, to grasp the lady's meaning. He lived and died in an age when men had a healthy preference for young and handsome rather than for gracious and gray-haired women (*vide* Burke on Marie Antoinette); but not even the youngest and handsomest could have sharpened the keenness of political strife. The begums were doubtless gray-haired if not gracious; but they were comfortably remote, and belonged to the world of abstractions like an after-dinner toast. The dramatist who held up to scorn 'an old maid verging on the desperation of six-and-thirty' had no use for mature charms save when associated with affectionate and capable wifehood. Sheridan married twice. He was fairly fortunate in both ventures.

In the year 1794, when the great three days' speech before the High Court of Parliament enthralled Londoners, a fellow of New College, Oxford, named Sydney Smith, took orders because it was the only means of livelihood open to him. Sheridan, the wit, left the field in which he stood unrivalled to follow the flame of his ambition. Sydney Smith, the wit, left the field of law, which he coveted, and accepted work which was alien to his spirit. He made the best — a very shining best — of it all his life.

What more can a man do? Sydney's tastes were as extravagant as Sheridan's. He loved the pleasant things of life as well as did Sheridan. 'My idea of Heaven,' he said in an imprudent moment, 'is eating *pâtés de foie gras* to the sound of trumpets.' Yet poverty failed to cost him his self-respect. He begged from no man, borrowed from no man, owed no man a shilling, and managed — Heaven knows how — to pay a debt of thirty pounds, which his brother

Courtenay had contracted at Winchester, out of his Fellow-
ship income of one hundred pounds. His exuberant gaiety
('He is the gayest man as well as the greatest wit in England,'
said Jeffrey), which militated against his weight as a churchman, would have been equally out of place in a barrister.
The higher reaches of the law are ponderous. His laugh was
infectious, but he laughed too much. 'To a dissenter like
myself,' said Harriet Martineau, 'there was something very
painful in the tone always taken by Sydney Smith about
Church matters.' But Miss Martineau's immense seriousness was humour-proof, and she liked to do more than her
share of talking. Sydney confessed that his recurrent night-
mare was being chained to a rock, and being talked to —
or at — by Macaulay and Harriet Martineau.

If dining-out had been a profession, Sydney Smith would
have stood at the head of it. His arrival at a dinner was
hailed with rejoicings. He looked precisely what he was.
The admirable canvas by Briggs might have been entitled
'Portrait of a *Bon Vivant*.' Naturally no prime minister could
visualize him as a bishop. Lord Grey knew the soundness of
his theology, and the value of his political services; but he
also knew the weight of visualization. He offered in place
of a bishopric the Residentiary Canonry of Saint Paul's
Cathedral ('A snug thing, let me tell you'), which brought
to the rector of Combe Florey an additional income of two
thousand pounds for doing just what he liked best to do —
live for three months of the year in London, and preach now
and then a sensible and gentlemanly sermon. Yet the great
city offered many pleasures to which he was singularly indifferent. He abhorred music, cared little for art, being just
sufficiently interested to prefer a bad picture to a good one,

and, strangest loss of all, disliked the drama, which ought
to have brought him enjoyment. 'I should not care if there
were no theatre in the world,' he said. He learned to read
Dickens, observing wisely that the soul of Hogarth had
entered into the body of Dickens; but he missed a great deal
— the rare perfection of Pecksniff, for example; a character
drawn for our true delight, who should, by every ruling of
art and nature, have been left secure in the seats of the
mighty.

Sydney Smith's common sense was so broad, so deep, so
steadfast that it reached the domain of wisdom. He com-
bined the reasonableness and stability of the eighteenth century with the humane aspirations of the nineteenth; and if
he were not always consistent, that was because nobody ever
is, or ever has been. His aversion to cruelty was as all-
embracing as Huxley's; he exempted no form of sport which
brought pain to bird or beast; but his sympathy for poachers
must have made him forget the pitiless traps in which they
snared their prey; and his dream of eating *pâtés de foie gras*
to the sound of trumpets ignored the calculated barbarity
which produced the food he loved. Saintsbury compared
his passion for justice to Voltaire's, giving the palm for simplicity and sincerity to the Englishman who was uncontam-
inated by personal vanity. 'A free altar and an open road
to Heaven' was his slogan, and it would have been hard to
find a better. His sermons were excellent, but he never
expected to hold congregations spellbound. He granted
them the privilege of distraction. 'A sparrow fluttering
about a church is an antagonist which the most profound
theologian in Europe is wholly unable to overcome.'

There he was wrong. He was always wrong when he

dealt offhand with matters beyond his ken. The Tullamore cat, that leaped from the rafters onto a woman's head and ran over the shoulders of the congregation, failed to distract the men and women who were listening to John Wesley. 'None of them cried out any more than if it had been a butterfly.' Sydney Smith's distaste for Methodists was as strong as his distaste for Quakers. He considered them both unreasonable, and reason and religion were to him synonymous terms. But he could not divine the strength of a current by standing on its brink, and he could not be brought to believe that the leadership of men is seldom the reward of intelligence.

And what of the laughter which was his perquisite as a wit? It trailed him through life, and was too closely associated with his name. How did it happen that Sheridan's laugh was rare and sardonic, and Sydney's frequent and jovial? Sheridan had to desert the drama and enter Parliament to be as condemnatory as he chose. Sydney, who had a pulpit from which to safely censure, and Swift before him as a model, felt no inclination for the task. The sense of comedy in life was too strong for him. He saw the world as Vanity Fair with a background of cruelty and the stake waiting for Faithful, but with absurdities well to the fore. His lightest sayings are the most amusing. He went to see Newton's portrait of Moore, and observed gravely to the artist: 'Couldn't you contrive to throw into his face a stronger expression of hostility to the Church establishment?' He fed his pigs on some fermented grain, not wishing to waste it, and was pleased to report them as 'happy in their sty, grunting the National Anthem.' He said that the attempt to heat Saint Paul's Cathedral was like trying to heat the county of Middlesex. Occasionally there is no visible desire to be funny, only a juxtaposition of ideas which lends humour to a casual remark. 'My brother Courtenay,' he mused, 'has, I am told, a hundred and fifty thousand pounds, and he keeps only a cat.' This was the brother whose debt of thirty pounds Sydney paid at Oxford; this was the brother whose death left him a rich man (the cat apparently did not inherit); and this was the brother to whom he said: 'We both of us illustrate contradictions in nature. You rise by your weight, and I fall by my levity.'

Which proves that the lost bishopric, while never essential to Sydney Smith's happiness of heart, was ever present in his mind. It was the price he paid for laughter.

VI

THE LAUGH THAT FAILED

Pleasure is not a programme. It exists here and there, for me and for no one else, once and never again.

GEORGE SANTAYANA

VI

THE LAUGH THAT FAILED

ONE night in June, 1804, an English boy of sixteen asked his father to listen to a song. The lad was charming to look at, fair-skinned, dark-haired, with sparkling blue eyes. He sang a gay little ditty, and he sang it as though he were laughing. The father, a musical composer of merit, listened with manifest delight. 'I have another,' said the boy, and sang again; this time a plaintive ballad, the words dropping like sighs from his lips.

'Who wrote the songs?' asked the father.

'I did,' answered the lad.

'And where did you find the airs?'

'I composed them.'

The father leaped from his chair. This prodigy was his son. This lad, hitherto shut up with ordinary English boys in a schoolroom at Harrow, held potential music in his brain and lungs. Of course he should not go back to the school he hated. Of course he should stay at home, and develop his talents under parental supervision. The mother was dead. An older brother was away from home. There was no one to intervene, and at sixteen Theodore Hook's fate was sealed.

The mischief so inauspiciously begun grew more perilous

111

every year. At seventeen young Hook was earning fifty pounds a week by composing songs for comic operas. He was spending guineas when he should have been saving shillings. He was behind the scenes in the theatres, where he began to show his remarkable powers of mimicry, and where he was tolerated for the fun he made. His brother strove valiantly to stem this merry current of life, and succeeded in getting him entered for Oxford. This was as far as his education ever went. In place of the stiff course of studies laid out for him, he composed two musical comedies which enjoyed more success than they deserved, and wrote a novel which was published and read. The curse of easy success lasted until he was twenty-five. It was like one of the spells cast by the malign fairies of our childhood.

A natural result was a flow of animal spirits which made the fortunate young man engage in elaborate jests — jests which seemed to him worth perpetrating, and which by their very vastness have become historic. He began by gate-crashing; not the common process of today, which means getting into a house only to be put out again. When Hook crashed a gate, he assumed a character and played a part. As the character was well chosen and the part well played, he was dined and wined and made much of by a flattered or an anxious host. It must be remembered that the kind of jokes which are now called 'practical' were then immensely popular. The Prince Regent loved them. They reached the level of his intelligence. When king, he played one on the old Duke of Norfolk; plying him with drink at table, driving him round and round the Pavilion lawn at Brighton when he thought he was returning to Arundel, and finally tucking him into a Pavilion bed, where he wakened in the morning. Thackeray explodes with wrath over this exploit, which was ill-bred and unkind, but of no great consequence. It seems an unconsidered trifle when compared to Hook's gigantic folly, commonly known as the Berners Street hoax.

So far as we are aware, there was no animating motive for this historic tomfoolery; 1809 was the year, and the neat appearance of a house on Berners Street — the home, as it chanced, of a well-to-do and childless widow — presented the occasion. 'I'll lay you a guinea,' said Hook to a companion, 'that in one week that nice modest dwelling shall be the most famous in London.' The bet was taken, and Hook went to work. Within five days he and his colleagues wrote letters (Lockhart says one thousand, Garnett says four) to tradesmen all over London. They ordered every kind of goods from coals and wood to books and prints, from potatoes and wines and brandies to jellies and cranberry tarts. All were to be sent at the same hour of the same day to the Berners Street address. Other letters of a more laborious character went to high officials, and revealed Hook's marvellous powers of imposition. The Lord Mayor and his chaplain were summoned to take the deathbed statement of a dishonest councilman. The chairman of the East India Company, a cabinet minister, a bishop, and — incredible though it may sound — the Duke of York, Commander-in-Chief of the British army, were urged, for reasons pious, patriotic, or personal, to present themselves at the 'modest' house on Berners Street. Philanthropists, popular preachers, and hairdressers were not forgotten.

Happily there were cautious tradesmen who — harbouring doubts about payment — ignored the call. But Hook was always convincing. Most of the people to whom he wrote responded, or endeavoured to respond. They blocked the narrow lanes that led to Berners Street. The military promptness of the Duke of York brought him early to the widow's door. With him and after him came carriages, wagons, and carts innumerable. As the hour wore on, the congestion became appalling. It was a field-day for the rabble. Battles were fought at every corner. There was a general smashing of all that was breakable, a free distribution of everything that could be eaten or drunk. Cases of wine and kegs of beer refreshed the thirsty. Horses were killed and men were injured. When the streets were cleared they looked like a battle-field.

Hook and a couple of friends had secured for themselves lodgings opposite the Berners Street house, and they watched in safety the development of the hoax, which exceeded their expectations. If there were any amusement to be derived from the performance, that amusement was theirs. They had worked hard enough for it, Heaven knows. They had pursued laughter so furiously that only a sense of exhaustion was left. Judged by their standard the joke was a good one, for the sufferers were many, and much indignation was aroused. Hook fell under immediate suspicion, and slipped out of London for a few weeks; but his secret was kept until he chose to divulge it; and two years later we find him again engaged in providing discomfort for others.

This time the jest consisted in forging a facsimile of the cards which invited the Prince Regent's guests to a magnificent fête at Carlton House. The card was sent to Mr. Coates, an amateur actor who was then squandering his money by renting the Haymarket, and playing Romeo on its boards. Coates repaired to Carlton House, where the Private Secretary spied him, suspected what had happened, and slipped him discreetly from the royal presence. The Regent, though his taste in jokes was not impeccable, was deeply displeased when he heard what had happened. He said he regretted that a man who had come to his doors in good faith should have been expelled from them; and he sent his Secretary to Mr. Coates the next day to express his regret and offer apologies.

All this time Hook, while admittedly a brilliant talker and the delight of the theatrical world, had never aspired to enter that other world of rank and fashion, which stood sorely in need of entertainment. But the time was at hand, and the occasion was a dinner given by the Drury Lane Company to its 'brilliant proprietor and irregular pay-master,' Mr. Sheridan. Hook, a young man of twenty-three, was at hand, and was called on to improvise some verses descriptive of the feast. It was an art in which he excelled, and in which he had no English rival. In the gayest mood and with perfect ease he rattled off his rhymes, praising or satirizing the distinguished guests, and weaving into his stanzas anything of a diverting nature that had happened during the dinner, or had been said by the diners. This *tour de force* stunned Sheridan, and enraptured his son, Tom. The two young men struck up a friendship which was destined to have serious results.

Hook's method of entertaining was certainly unique. Lockhart describes an evening in the house of a gay bachelor who lived near Highgate. Coleridge was one of the guests. All had dined, and all were apparently drunk. Hook at the piano sang bacchanalian songs of his own composition in which Coleridge figured largely. The room was full and stiflingly hot. Hook suddenly rose, and sent his empty glass crashing through a window pane. Coleridge rose in turn, and with an aspect of solemn benignancy sent his glass hurtling through another pane. Guest after guest followed suit. It was a grand night for the glaziers. The host was farthest from the windows. His goblet smashed the chandelier. Hook sat down again, and rattled off an improvised ballad about the goodness and badness of the shots. Coleridge, overcome by admiration and by punch, pronounced him a genius, as great as Dante, only different.

The rise of this genius in the social world was rapid. Tom Sheridan presented him to the Marchioness of Hertford, who in turn brought him to the notice of the Prince Regent; and that august arbiter pronounced judgment in his favour. At the first meeting he said, 'Mr. Hook I must see and hear you again.' At the second he said, 'Something must be done for Hook.' At the third or fourth he was so richly entertained that the favourite's fortune was assured. In November, 1812, he was appointed Accountant General and Treasurer to the Colony of the Mauritius, a much-coveted post, which carried a salary and allowances amounting to two thousand pounds a year.

Hook was not yet twenty-five. His qualifications for public service were a ready wit, a good tenor voice, a sweet temper, a talent for improvisation, and an unstinted enjoyment of every form of pleasure. He was fairly intelligent, but imperfectly educated, with no experience of, or aptitude for, business. Of course he was delighted with Mauritius, and of course Mauritius was delighted with him. The island was an earthly Paradise; 'every hour seems happier than the last.' The Accountant General may have known nothing of accounts; but he was a charming host, a good sport, a lover of the turf, and friendly to all classes. Be it remembered to his credit that he paid off his English debts within two years; but he could not grow rich in a place where the cost of living was so unevenly distributed. 'Fresh butter at ten shillings a pound, and fifteen shillings for a pair of gloves; but good claret at tenpence a bottle, and pineapples a penny apiece. Necessities are exorbitant, luxuries dirt cheap, and a pretty life we do lead.'

How this life managed to run on for nearly five years, Heaven alone knows. It came to an abrupt close in January, 1817, when William Allan, a mulatto clerk in the Treasury Office, wrote to Lieutenant Governor Hall reporting a deficit of twelve thousand pounds. This was an announcement too startling to be disregarded, and an investigation followed. The books were found to be in great disorder, which might have been expected; but there was absolutely no evidence to show that Hook had appropriated the money. There was, in fact, no evidence to show anything. The twelve thousand pounds had disappeared, and nobody — least of all the Accountant General — knew what had become of them. The 'haughty vagueness' of his replies to all inquiries was not helpful; and when, three weeks after writing his letter, Allan shot himself, the last clue was lost.

What followed was a compromise. Hook was not accused of peculation; but was declared to be a debtor to the British Government for the money which had been supposedly under his guardianship. His property in Mauritius was

seized, and there is a touching story of a Negro slave who
boarded the ship on which the deposed Treasurer was
returning to England, and begged his acceptance of his
own writing-desk, which this humble friend had bought at
auction for ten shillings that he might have the happiness
of restoring it. Back in London with only two gold mohurs
in his pocket, and a mountain of debt (which did not weigh
very heavily because not a shilling of it was ever to be paid)
hanging over his head, Hook, with the dexterity of a cat,
landed squarely on his feet. The Tory periodical, *John
Bull*, devoted to the interests of the King and the vilifica-
tion of the Queen, was started in 1820. To him was
assigned the editorship, with permission to be as ribald as he
chose.

It was a large order, amply fulfilled. If the royal consorts
were hard to praise, they were easy to censure. *John Bull*
stopped at nothing in the way of insult; but its blazing
audacity of invective never degenerated into dull abuse.
In fact it was never dull at all:

Tous les gens sont permis hors les gens ennuyeux.

If its swift prose and rattling rhymes carry little meaning
to us today, that is because dead issues cannot be re-enlivened.
In its time the paper was of real service to the King; and
incidentally it yielded its editor — who did all the work —
an income of two thousand pounds, as much as he had received at Mauritius, and with no attendant expenses.

Of course this could not last, but while it continued,
Hook was at the height of his fortune. When he first returned to England he was held in custody, and forced to
reside within the precincts of the sheriff's office. When

freed from this restriction (apparently because there was no earthly use in holding him), it was with the warning that he was still a debtor to the Crown — a circumstance which he was not permitted to forget. He took a cottage at Putney, and gradually regained his old position in the social world. His perversity in living with a woman whom he would neither marry for the sake of his children (he had five of them), nor abandon for the sake of himself, closed his own doors to the polite world, but left him free to enter the doors of others. His debt made it impossible for him to hold property, but permitted him to spend an ample income. He was a hard and a quick worker, publishing thirty-eight books in sixteen years, which was far too many. They sold well, the three series of 'Sayings and Doings' being the most successful. As he grew too fashionable for Putney, he moved to what he called 'real London,' became a member of exclusive clubs, and was deeply appreciated in all of them. When he made a habit of dining at the Athenaeum, scores of members dined there on the chance of hearing him talk. When he disappeared from his accustomed corner, the attendance dropped.

Strange to say, this consummate actor had a fixed and rooted aversion for the stage, and a contempt for the profession of acting. Yet he was a thing of unreality, playing a part which became more distasteful every year. Garnett calls him a 'hired jester,' but it is a question how a man who is unpaid can be said to be hired. It was precisely because he did not have to be paid that he was for some years the most popular diner-out in London. The hostess who sent her little daughter around the table at the second course to beg Hook to 'begin to be funny' took this shameless liberty because she was getting, or hoped to get, something for nothing. The jester who was not jesting must be reminded of his task. He went his way to the sound of laughter; but his inborn gaiety of heart was growing faint. His personal debts were beginning to threaten his daily bread, and his debt to the Crown forever shadowed his honour. There was no dignity in his life, and no just cause for self-respect. Sydney Smith also went laughing — half against his will — through the world; but Sydney Smith stood on firm ground, the equal of his associates, an independent churchman and a very admirable English gentleman. Hook was an air plant. He had no roots. He had no sure income. He behaved like a man of wealth and a man of pleasure when he was neither, and every year his position became more untenable.

There were good traits in this drifter with the tide. He is said to have been the original of Mr. Wagg in 'Vanity Fair' and 'Pendennis'; but if this be true, Thackeray went wide of the mark. Hook was never contemptible, and Wagg was never anything else. Hook was capable of sustained kindness which to Wagg would have seemed preposterous. When an old theatrical friend, Michael Kelly, put together some odds and ends of reminiscences, he asked Hook to help him in getting them published. Hook made sure of this consummation by rewriting every chapter, infusing into each vitality and fun. The book was received with amazement (Kelly had never been considered a wit), and Hook kept his own counsel. If a more generous deed than this was ever done, the world should be ringing with its fame.

Byron spared a kind and wise word anent Hook's early

flights. He mocked in 'English Bards and Scotch Reviewers' at the absurd and melodramatic 'Tekeli':

> Puns and a prince within a barrel pent;

but he recognized its author as a man of talent engaged in wasting his powers. No one knew better than Byron the peril of success that is won too soon and too cheaply. He, too, had flashed meteor-like across the world of letters.

Like many other men who are compelled to write ceaselessly for a living, Hook devoted his spare moments to filling up pages in a diary. Scott, who every morning held a pen until it slipped from his numb fingers, sat down at night and scrawled passages as gay and as poignant as any in his novels. They were meant for his own delectation and solace; but we could no more spare his description of himself as a 'pebble-hearted cur' parting dry-eyed from the susceptible Mme. Mirbel than we could spare 'The Heart of Midlothian.' Hook's diary is as bleak as if it had been written in a Siberian prison. It tells the story of his losses at play, his losses in lotteries, the pressure of his unpaid bills. It tells of visits to the houses of peers, where he flung about his last guineas, and had nothing to show for them but his name in the 'fashionable intelligence.' It affords material in plenty for a moral essay or for a sermon; but from first to last it is innocent of gaiety. Its author never wasted a joke upon himself.

And this brings us to the consideration of a problem. What has become of all the jests, all the witticisms, all the brilliant repartees and laughter-provoking comments with which we are told Theodore Hook strewed his social path? A formidable volume has been compiled of Sydney Smith's best — and worst — sayings. A lesser volume might be compiled of Sheridan's. But Lockhart in fifty-five closely printed pages tells just one well-known and amusing story which relates to Hook's early youth. When he was seventeen, his clerical brother escorted him to Oxford to be matriculated. The Vice Chancellor asked him if he were prepared to sign the Thirty-Nine Articles. 'Yes, sir,' said the boy. 'Forty, if you like.' The jest all but cost him his matriculation, not being to the taste of the authorities, and only his brother's ample apologies saved the day. But there is a quality of wit and a quality of sense about it. Forty has always seemed a natural, and thirty-nine an unnatural, number of anything. 'Ali Baba and the Thirty-Nine Thieves' would never have been the deathless story that it is.

Hook's novels were overrated in their day, and have perished since. Lockhart, whose literary perspective was a bit 'early,' risked saying that he was 'the only male novelist of his time, except Mr. Dickens, who has drawn portraits of contemporary English society destined for permanent existence'; and made no doubt that the best of his work would 'go down' with Miss Austen and Miss Edgeworth. It is a curious circumstance that the critics of the early nineteenth century, who all knew that Jane Austen's novels were good, never recognized them as supreme. They felt that they honoured their author when they placed her by Miss Edgeworth's side.

Hook died, a prematurely old man, at fifty-three. Only in London, where tradesmen do not expect, and apparently have never expected, to be paid, could his debts have multiplied so enormously. A student of life's ironies should be aware that the father of John Horne Tooke, the philologist, was a decent poulterer who once accommodated Frederick, Prince of Wales, in the matter of a right-of-way. The gratified Hanoverian appointed him poulterer to his household, and, dying some years later, owed him several thousand pounds, which the tradesman was never able to collect. The sale of Theodore Hook's library and effects brought twenty-five hundred pounds, which went to the Crown as preferred creditor. He had always hoped that this debt would be wiped out in consideration of his services to the King's party, which was a not unreasonable expectation. On the other hand, he had never, when in possession of a large income, made any effort to lessen his indebtedness, which would have been the natural action of a man who held his honour high. The Lords of the Treasury, hardened by his unconcern, absorbed the twenty-five hundred pounds, and his widow and children, like the tradesmen, went bare.

A subscription was opened for them to which the King of Hanover (Ernest, Duke of Cumberland) sent five hundred pounds; but it never reached an adequate sum. The British public has always entertained a prejudice against illicit relations. Charles the Second was aware of this circumstance when he said, 'Let not poor Nelly starve!' and so was Nelson when he made his dying appeal to his country to be generous to Lady Hamilton. It is true that both these light-o'-loves were reduced to poverty by their own absurd extravagance; but neither of them had been brought up wisely and well. Nell melted her plate, and James the Second paid her debts, and she learned to live thriftily, and left money to the poor when she died. But Lady Hamilton had no friend at court. England cordially disapproved of her; but the fact remains that although she was fat and foolish (qualities fatal to romance) she was — next to this same unforgiving England — the thing that Nelson held most dear. By virtue of this circumstance she counted for more at Trafalgar than did his clerical brother upon whom were lavished all the undeserved rewards — a peerage, a pension of five thousand pounds, and ninety thousand pounds to purchase an estate.

With these shining examples before their eyes, the friends of Theodore Hook could not have hoped for a generous response to their subscription. The entries in his diary show that in the last years of his life he was deeply concerned over the youth and helplessness of his children; but it is characteristic of such men that they begin to grieve when it is too late to do anything else. Hook must have looked back bitterly upon his own merry, careless, and absurdly affluent boyhood when he sent his elder son, a lad of fifteen, to India, to fight his way with a cadetship, the gift of an old friend. He must have remembered that life, which promised hardships in plenty for this young adventurer, had for him dawned too brightly. He had dared to frame a programme of pleasure, only to find, without the aid of philosophy, that pleasure has its own law of being. He had stirred the world — his world — to laughter, and, like Grimaldi, he had no other method of approach. Pope saw us moving angels to tears by our absurdities. Horace Walpole saw us moving them to laughter. The absurdities are ever the same. Only the audience differs.

VII

THE HOUSE OF LAUGHTER

La Gaieté est près de la bonté

VII

THE HOUSE OF LAUGHTER

It was rather a famous house, and Sir James Mackintosh once proposed to write its history; but lost his zeal when he found how much there was to tell. It stood sedately in Kensington; and in 1873 Macmillan published two quarto volumes, presenting its glories to the world through the medium of steel engravings, woodcuts, and heliogravures. General Fairfax lived in it, and Addison died in it. Van Dyck and William Penn were among its tenants. Charles James Fox should have been born in it, but wasn't, because Lady Caroline found the neighbourhood too noisy, and preferred less august and more restful quarters for her confinement.

To this historic mansion, renovated and adorned with architectural furbelows, Henry Richard Fox, third Lord Holland, brought in 1796 the lady who was first his mistress and afterwards his honoured and obeyed wife. Her maiden name was Elizabeth Vassall, and she had been married at sixteen to Sir Godfrey Webster of Battle Abbey, Sussex. She possessed some beauty, large estates in Jamaica, an imperious temper, and a quick tongue. Lord Holland, who had reached the mature age of twenty-one, met her in Florence (she was four years his senior), and carried her back with him to England. Sir Godfrey, who gave no indication of a broken heart, divorced her in the leisurely English fashion;

and, after the birth of a son, she was married to her lover in the parish church of Rickmansworth. Forty-three years of domestic harmony followed this seemingly ill-advised union.

No house could have been too big or too showy for Lady Holland. She revealed from the first a taste and a talent for entertaining which fitted her hospitable instincts, but were at variance with her incorrigible self-assertiveness. It was the good fortune of Englishmen in the beginning of the nineteenth century to find themselves free to dine, and glad to dine, with a hostess whose youthful indiscretion gave them a solid British excuse for leaving their wives at home. In the course of years the London world forgot all about this indiscretion ('Lady Holland sinned early in life with Methuselah and Enoch,' wrote Sydney Smith to Lord Denman); but in the beginning she was forced to content herself with the companionship of brilliant and agreeable men who were presumed to remain untarnished by her proximity.

Of Lord Holland nothing but good was spoken. During the long years of Tory ascendancy, when there was 'no more chance of a Whig Administration than of a thaw in Nova Zembla,' he held the party together, and made of it a disturbing minority. His opinions were crystallized into a textbook of Whig domestic policy. Oppression sanctioned by law was his peculiar horror, and it was his fate in life to make little headway against it. Imprisonment for debt at the will and pleasure of the creditor seemed to him as detestable as slavery in the West Indies. The Corn Laws were cruel, but so was capital punishment for minor offences. He supported Catholic Emancipation, an unpopular measure in the House of Lords, and he protested vehemently, but vainly, against St. Helena as a place of detention for Napoleon.

Now how could a man who spent his life tilting against the cherished abuses of power maintain an unbroken cheerfulness of demeanour, and an even flow of spirits? 'In my whole experience of our race,' said Lord Brougham, 'I never saw such a temper, nor anything that at all resembled it.' 'Holland,' said Lord John Russell, 'won without seeming to court, instructed without seeming to teach, and amused without labouring to be witty.' 'There is no human being,' wrote Lord Byron to Rogers, 'on whose regard and esteem I set a higher value than on Lord Holland's.' He at least had proved the sincerity of his words.

Why the *Edinburgh Review* should have deemed it worth while to write long disparaging pages about Byron's 'Hours of Idleness' can be explained only on the supposition that the harmless nothings of a peer were thought to deserve more notice, and consequently more condemnation, than the harmless nothings of a commoner. Why Byron should have imagined that Lord Holland had inspired the article can be explained only on a similar assumption — that one peer fancied himself of importance to another. As it chanced, Holland had never seen the verses, and had never heard of the poet, being under the impression that the title was extinct. Naturally it was a shock to him, when 'English Bards and Scotch Reviewers' took London by storm, to find himself, his wife, and most of his friends held up to ridicule in its pages. He, indeed, escaped lightly as the host who fed Grub Street; but there was an ugly jab at Lady Holland, to whom was ascribed the unlikely duties of a moral censor. Her business was to save the *Review* from masculine coarseness, to

> Breathe o'er the page her purity of soul,
> Reform each error and refine the whole.

Never was there so rough a pathway to a lifelong friendship. When Byron was well assured that Lord and Lady Holland had been unaware of his very existence, and when he had recovered his characteristic reasonableness which the petulance of youth had obscured, he asked Lord Holland what he had better do to make amends. Holland, who did not hold with half measures, advised him strongly to withdraw the satire from circulation. Byron, who was then hard at work revising a fifth edition, acceded promptly to this demand. He wrote to his publishers, and bade them destroy all the copies on their shelves. A few escaped, which inevitably happens. Dallas retained two. One passed into Murray's hands, and furnished the text for the edition of 1831. Another reposes serenely on the shelves of the British Museum.

It is easier to start a blaze than to extinguish it. 'English Bards and Scotch Reviewers' was more like a bonfire than a conflagration, but it would not be put out. In 1813 Byron wrote in his journal: 'I wish I had not been in such a hurry with that confounded satire, of which I would suppress even the memory. But people, now that they can't get it, make a fuss, I verily believe out of contrariety.' Four years later he wrote to Murray, authorizing him to republish any of his poems in a large edition, with the solitary exception of 'English Bards.' To revive 'that foolish lampoon' would be, he considered, idiocy. 'Not for any consideration would I do so. It is not good for much, even in the way of verse; and you are to recollect that I gave up its republication on account of the Hollands. I do not think that time or circumstances can neutralize this suppression.'

Holland House was not in Byron's day the pre-eminent

130

LAUGHTER

social centre it afterwards became; but it was shaping itself in that direction, and had already assumed, for good or bad, its distinguishing characteristics. Lady Holland cared nothing for the comfort or convenience of her guests. She crowded them at table — sixteen when there was barely space for nine — and urged them to 'make room.' 'It will certainly have to be made,' said Luttrell, 'for it does not exist.' She froze them because she was insensitive to cold. This was Byron's especial grievance, and he confided it to the pages of his journal in November, 1813: 'Why does Lady H. always have that damned screen between the whole room and the fire? I, who bear cold no better than an antelope, was absolutely petrified, and could not even shiver. All the rest looked as if they were just unpacked, like salmon from an ice-basket, and set down to table for that day only. When she retired, I watched their looks as I dismissed the screen, and every cheek thawed, and every nose reddened with the anticipated glow.'

If Byron had kicked over the screen before his hostess had left the dining-room, she would probably have forgiven him, for he was the *enfant gâté* of the establishment. Always an agreeable companion ('cheerful, frank, and witty,' said Shelley), there was in him a rush of inborn vitality like an Alpine torrent. Scott, who like the Hollands had something to forgive, forgave with all his heart. He had, as it chanced, no great fancy for wits; but delighted in companionship that was both grave and gay. 'Byron,' he wrote, 'occasionally said what are called good things, but he never strove for them. They came naturally and easily, and mixed with the comic or the serious as it happened.'

That there was real affection between the spoiled hostess

and her spoiled guest does not admit of a doubt. Byron dedicated to her 'The Bride of Abydos,' by way of atonement for his early errors, and commented more than once in his journal upon her kindness and her charm. Shortly after the episode of the screen he wrote: 'Dined last night with Lord Holland. Lady Holland in perfect good humour, and consequently perfect. No one more agreeable, or perhaps so much so, when she will.' As for the lady's sentiments, they were expressed with feeling and simplicity after the wasted death at Missolonghi. Moore asked her if she thought Lady Byron had ever really loved her husband. 'She must have done so,' was the impetuous reply. 'He was so lovable.'

These friends saw each other at his and her best because the period of their friendship coincided with the most sane and reasonable years of their lives. 'Byron,' said George Meredith, 'had splendid powers of humour, and the most poetic satire of which we have any example, fusing at times to hard irony. He had no strong comic sense, or he would not have taken an anti-social position.' But he did not take an anti-social position until after his unfortunate marriage, and he displayed a broad-blown comic sense in all that appertained to the most amusing episode of his life — his connection with Drury Lane. He was a diligent member of the Sub-Committee of Management, which sounds humble (all subs do), but which gave him plenty of experience. The theatre had been burned down and rebuilt. When Samuel Whitbread, brewer, politician, and manager, died by his own hand, it was said that the anxieties and disputes attendant to the rebuilding and reorganization had driven him to suicide — 'a consolatory encouragement to the new Committee,' observed Byron.

Whitbread lived long enough, however, to deliver the address when Drury Lane was reopened in 1812. Byron wrote a poem for the occasion, and with perfect good humour consented to have it corrected and curtailed by the management. On one point only he was resolute. He would not — though it seemed inevitable — compare the theatre risen from its ashes to the phoenix. 'How am I to avoid it?' he said to Holland. 'We must not for the world have a feather of that damned bird which is become as commonplace as the turtle-dove.' He was offered, and declined, a quiet hiding-place whence he could hear his poem declaimed. 'Not for the universe,' he said, 'would I be — if I could help it — within fifty miles of the spot that night.' 'It was well he was not there,' commented Holland. 'Mr. Elliston recited the lines in a manner that would drive any poet mad.'

To confess the truth, no grace of delivery could have made Byron's address anything but insipid. The comments of the press were cold and critical, and it was saved from utter damnation only by the fact that Whitbread's address managed to be worse. He at least revelled in the phoenix, and described it minutely for the benefit of those who might not have been familiar with its system of survivals. 'Byron at least wrote like a poet,' said Holland, 'and Whitbread like a schoolboy.' 'Not like a schoolboy,' corrected Sheridan; 'like a poulterer.'

Apparently the only glint of gaiety which enlivened the audience that night was afforded by Miss Farren, who in the interval between *Macbeth* and a farce, *The Virgin Unmasked*, explained in fluent rhyme the safety secured by an iron curtain which in the event of another fire could be rapidly lowered, cutting off the stage — where conflagrations started — from the house:

> Now we assure our generous benefactors
> 'Twill only burn the scenery and the actors.

It is a curious episode in the history of English letters that the opening of Drury Lane, which made Byron dull and Whitbread duller, should have been perpetuated by that masterpiece of travesty, *Rejected Addresses*, which took London by storm. Most of the poets it mocked were among its most ardent admirers. Scott insisted that he must have written the parody on 'Marmion,' although he could not remember when or why:

> 'Whitford and Mitford ply your pumps,
> You Clutterbook, come stir your stumps,
> A fireman, and afraid of bumps!
> What are they fear'd on? fools! 'od rot 'em!'
> Were the last words of Higginbottom.

Byron, as appreciative as Scott, wrote to Murray: 'You should have published that little book. I wish it all success. Its author is a man of lively wit, and much less scurrilous than wits often are.' As a matter of fact it did pass — by the time it had reached its eighteenth edition — into the hands of that wise, generous, and profoundly patient publisher, who used to tell with delight the story of a Leicestershire clergyman who said to him that he did not see why all the addresses should have been rejected: 'Some of them were very good.'

Byron loved the stage. He confessed that he never could resist a first night, not even when he should have stayed at home because his wife's uncle was dead; and not even when he feared, with reason, that the play would be damned. Those were the days when the pit, if it were displeased or badly bored, rose and roared the actors down, making their voices inaudible. Byron, who had no more liking for the tyranny of the mob than for the tyranny of politicians or of Turks, hated these crude manifestations of displeasure. He sat cowering in the back of his box when Mrs. Wilmot's tragedy *Ina* failed unequivocally. The first three acts 'oozed patiently but heavily on.' Even Kean could do nothing to vitalize them. Throughout the fourth the house showed ominous signs of impatience. Byron shrank more deeply into the shadows. Midway in the fifth act, when the hero was saying his prayers, the pit, 'the damnable pit,' rose on its legs and howled defiance. The poet slipped out of the theatre, more than ever convinced that women could not write tragedies. 'They have not seen enough, or felt enough, of life,' he reflected; and then bethought himself of Semiramis and Catherine the Second. 'Rare plays they might have written,' he said.

Byron's kindness to actors and dancers was as whimsical as Mr. Gilbert's. It was long remembered in New York that Gilbert, seeing one of the chorus girls in tears, asked her what was wrong. The girl replied that the dresser had told her she was 'no better than she ought to be.' 'But you *are* better than you ought to be, aren't you?' said the dramatist with sympathetic and serious conviction. Byron's efforts to keep the peace between a ballet-master who wished the *pas seul* to come in the middle of the dance, and the *première danseuse* who wished it to come at the close, were unsuccessful. After patient listening and reflection he decided in favour of the dancer, for the not very logical reason that she resembled Lady Jane Harley. 'Likenesses go a great way with me,' he admitted. The ballet-master, unmoved by, because ignorant of, this consideration, refused to accept defeat. The lady would not yield, and it was 'a devil of a row on and off the stage.'

On the whole, however, the cast was easier to manage than were the playwrights. Andrew Lang said that an editor was engaged 'in a kind of intellectual egg-dance among a score of sensitive interests.' But running a magazine is pastime compared to running a theatre, which is more like a sword-dance than a harmless diversion with eggs. When Byron became a sub-manager, he found over five hundred plays waiting to be read. Some of them, he thought, must be good. All of them, he found, were bad. Then scores of new plays were hurled at his head. Sir James Bland Burges sent him offhand four tragedies and a farce. A 'Miss Emma Somebody' brought him a drama entitled *The Bandit of Bohemia*, 'of which she thought well.' An unknown genius signing himself 'Hibernicus' sent him a tragedy called *Turgesius*, which he described in lively fashion to Moore: 'In the last act, Turgesius, a Dane and a usurper, is chained by the leg to a pillar. King Malachi, Irishman and hero, makes him a speech, not unlike Lord Castlereagh's, about the balance of power and the lawfulness of legitimacy, which puts Turgesius into a frenzy—as Castlereagh would if his audience were chained by the leg. He draws a dagger and rushes at the orator; but finding himself at the end of his tether, sticks it into his own body and dies, saying he has fulfilled a prophecy.'

Byron dealt gently with the author of this play, 'a wild man of a salvage aspect,' who came in person to the theatre, and filled him with justifiable apprehension. But in truth he was always as gentle as circumstances permitted. 'I am really a civil and polite person,' he said of himself, 'and do hate giving pain if it can be avoided.' When Mr. Betterton, a dancing-master of sixty and the father of Julia Betterton the actress, took it into his head that he could play Archer in Farquhar's comedy *The Beaux' Stratagem,* and called upon Byron 'dressed in silk stockings on a frosty morning to show his legs, which were certainly good, and Irish for his age, and had been still better,' the sub-manager soothed the old gentleman with compliments in place of compliance. His 'angel of reasonableness' stood him in good stead.

He relished the absurdities of the stage, he reverenced its traditions, and he had a discriminating taste. He noted in his journal, after seeing Kean as Richard III: 'Kemble's Hamlet is perfect, but Hamlet is not nature. Richard is a man, and Kean is Richard.' In 1804 'young Roscius,' otherwise William Betty, a boy of thirteen, was playing to crowded houses at Covent Garden and Drury Lane. So dense and so determined was the mob that the military was called out to preserve order. The critics were as mad as the mob. Even *John Bull* paused in its frenzied political diatribes to sing frenzied praises of the prodigy. In the midst of this turmoil, Byron, then in his seventeenth year, wrote calmly to his mother that the young actor was 'tolerable in some characters, but by no means deserving of the ridiculous praises showered upon him.'

What wonder that this brilliant and impulsive guest, who said good things without striving for them, should have been welcome to Lady Holland's table and dear to Lady Holland's heart? If he sometimes breathed an irritated word to her or about her, she forgave, knowing that, like a red Indian, he never forgot a kindness. His lifelong loyalty to Madame de Staël, who had few admirers in England, was an instance of this uncivilized trait. Moreover she relished his observations, laughed at his picture of Mr. Edgeworth, 'bouncing about, talking loud and long, active, brisk and endless'; and probably understood when he refused to dine with Mat Lewis (whom he liked) because his would-be host had 'looking-glass panels in his book-cases' — a sound excuse for any man of taste to stay away.

In 1816 Byron left England, and seven years later he wrote to Moore that Henry Fox, Lord Holland's second legitimate son, had paid him a visit in Genoa. He was strangely moved by the meeting. Old memories crowded his mind, old friendships tugged at his heart. 'The boy,' he wrote, 'has the softest and most amiable expression I ever saw, and his manners correspond. I speak from a transient glimpse; but I love still to yield to such impressions; for I have ever found that those I liked longest and best I took to at first sight. I always fancied that lad — perhaps from some resemblance in the less fortunate part of our destinies — I mean his lameness. But there is this difference, that he appears a halting angel who has tripped against a star, while I am *Le Diable Boiteux.*'

If Byron shone for a time in the outermost rim of the Holland House circle, its centre was composed — so say its historians — of a triad; Rogers, Luttrell, and Sydney Smith. All three were good Whigs, but Sydney alone was of any service to the party. All three were good talkers, and they were cherished for the sake of their conversation. This was as it should have been, for Lord Holland's dwelling-place was first and foremost a house of laughter — the lost laughter of

138

the Middle Ages, which it pursued and sometimes captured by means of a comic sense. It would never have served as a rallying-point in the long twilight of Whiggism if its atmosphere had been choleric, or depressing, or dull. Its master hated political diatribes as stoutly as he hated political abuses. Its mistress, although her religious convictions were intangible, suffered nothing that savoured of profanity. The one honest perplexity of her mind was the quarrelsomeness of creeds. 'This confounded division of the country into Protestant and Catholic,' she wrote to Lord John Russell, 'makes the King [George IV] as powerful as was Henry VIII. He is at present as anti-Catholic as was his father, and has assured the Archbishop that they may depend upon him as a Defender of the Faith.'

Lord Holland had a neat wit of his own and a gift of lively narrative. Nothing could be better than his account of going to Carlton House to hear a paper which the Prince of Wales had written on some Parliamentary question. Sheridan accompanied him, and told him that the Prince had drawn up the rough draft of this letter so badly that it could not be used; and that he, Sheridan, had recast the manuscript, leaving just enough of the original to enable the sensitive author to think it was still his own. Admitted to the royal presence, the Prince complacently produced the paper and said: 'Sheridan drew up a damned bad letter; but I just took his general outline, and changed it when needful.' He then proceeded to read impressively, turning every few minutes to Sheridan and saying: 'You know how that stood in your draft, but I altered it'; or: 'You will allow that is better than your rendering' — to all of which the renowned but submissive subject nodded assent. Holland left the room uncertain as to the authorship of the document, but quite sure that in either case it was valueless.

The outer circle of Holland House was a wide one, changing inevitably with the ebb and flow of London's social and political life. But in its centre, Rogers, Luttrell, and Sydney lived long unchallenged. Rogers supplied the poetic element. He was the darling of the reviewers, their one accepted versifier, their buttress against the strange encroachments of men like Wordsworth and Coleridge who were not without followers. He possessed also an acidulous wit, more feared than admired, and seemingly at variance with his boundless kindness and generosity. He it was who said it mattered little whom a man married, for he was sure to find the next morning that he had married somebody else. He did not in this instance speak from experience, but from a fear of experience, which is a great deterrent.

If Sydney Smith was the best beloved of the triad, Luttrell was by all odds the gayest, boldest, and most invincible. His wit flowed so readily that he outshone Sydney, who was apt to talk in character. He was known as a gourmet, a superbly independent Lucullus, who had learned to dine himself better than friends could dine him. Even his flights of fancy were gluttonous. Lord Holland was a portly gentleman, addicted to white waistcoats of breadth and volume. When he rose to answer a toast, Luttrell said he looked like a turbot standing on its tail. Sydney could laugh at Lady Holland, and, if there were need, could quarrel with her; but Luttrell routed her completely. He refused to enter her doors until she had suppressed a handsome and aggressive cat that had attacked Brougham and bitten Rogers. The lady loved best those pets that needed most defence; but in this case she surrendered with that sudden and flattering warmth of appeal which always won for her forgiveness.

For she was a woman who had to be forgiven a great deal. She did not hold with Heine that God has given us tongues in order that we may say pleasant things to our neighbours. She said unpleasant things by preference. Her rudest remarks were occasionally justified by truth, as when she told Moore that she feared his life of Sheridan would be a dull book; but it was certainly unreasonable in her to object to 'Lalla Rookh' because it was oriental. What else could it have been! 'Poets inclined to a plethora of vanity would find an occasional dose of Lady Holland very good for their complaint,' observed Moore, who had once trembled in her presence, but who had grown too popular and too sure of himself to care what any fine lady said about a poem which had brought him three thousand guineas and the applause of Europe. He even forgave Lord Melbourne the inconsiderate remark: 'I see there is a new edition of Crabbe coming out. It is a good thing when these authors die, for then one gets their works and is done with it.'

Like most unreasonable people, Lady Holland was easily quelled. It was her husband's habit of yielding to her whims which established her as a household tyrant. When she bade him do a thing, he did it to save trouble. But when she bade Lord Melbourne change his seat at dinner, that gentleman left the dining-room and the house without the formality of saying good-bye. When she bade Sydney Smith ring the bell, he asked lazily if he should sweep the floor. She met her match in one American, Mr. George Ticknor, whom she asked if the New England colonies had not been penal settlements. 'Your ladyship should know,' was the suave reply, 'for there were several Vassalls among the early inhabitants of Massachusetts, and there is a tablet to one of them in King's Chapel, Boston.'

Another foreigner, M. Van de Weyer, minister from Belgium, was equally quick-witted and equally urbane. At the dinner-table Lady Holland asked him suddenly, 'How is Leopold?' M. Van de Weyer, somewhat taken back by the wording of the inquiry, said, 'Does your Ladyship mean the King of the Belgians?' 'Belgians?' echoed his hostess scornfully. 'I have heard of Flemings, Hainaulters, and Brabanters; but Belgians are new to me.' 'Madame,' observed the diplomat gently, 'is it possible that in the course of your wide reading you have not come across a book written by a lad named Julius Cæsar? He was an able soldier who in his Commentaries gave to all our population the name of Belgians, which we have kept to this day.'

Lady Holland's most dextrous opponent was Talleyrand. Her incivility and variations of temper displeased a man whose sarcasms were — to use Lord Holland's expression — 'both courtly and careless.' He was sentiment-proof, and his Gallic mind rejected confused issues. It was no use telling him that his hostess had a good heart when what he objected to were her bad manners. He did not want to be reminded that she had been instrumental in getting a pension for Campbell, and the Yorkshire living for Sydney Smith, when she perversely advanced her dinner hour to five o'clock, '*pour gêner tout le monde.*' What puzzled him was the fact that this inconsiderate hostess was never short of guests. Why did they all go, and why did he — at widening intervals — go with them to her dinners? Why did the remarks of a woman who was neither wise nor witty command attention? '*Elle*

142

est toute assertion, mais quand on demande la preuve, c'est là son secret.'

Alone of all the guests of Holland House, Fanny Kemble cherished a resentment which never permitted her to forget or forgive Lady Holland's offences. The actress, herself imperious and self-centred, regarded with supreme distaste a woman whose imperiousness was harsher, and whose egotism was more overbearing, than her own. She represents herself as getting the better of her hostess in an encounter of wits, which might well have been the case; and she would have us believe that people went to the house only because of the esteem they bore its master. In this regard, she said what she desired to think rather than what she knew to be the fact. Her picture of the widowed Lady Holland as lonely and miserable is not borne out by circumstances. The Whigs had been too long in the habit of meeting at her table to forego that established rite. It had been the centre of their social life, the inspiration of their political exile. The peevish Greville confessed that there was 'nothing like it in Europe'; and we have Fanny Kemble's own words written in her diary before Lord Holland's death: 'The most perfect civilization could produce nothing better in the way of enjoyment than the intercourse of that delightful mansion.'

Perhaps political exile afforded a more auspicious atmosphere for Holland House than political ascendancy could have done. It was not in the power of any party triumph to disturb Lord Holland's mental equilibrium; but who could have said as much for his wife? 'What shall we do with Lady Holland in the Cabinet?' was Canning's way of putting it when there was talk of a change of ministry. The agitation over reform gave to the Whigs a spell of power in 1831.

Lord Holland was appointed Chancellor of the Duchy of Lancaster, a post which he held until he died in 1840. Lady Holland was by no means satisfied with this moderate reward for services. She remarked to Lord John Russell that she saw no reason why her husband should not be Secretary for Foreign Affairs, a post he was eminently qualified to fill. Russell, the kind of man who would have walked to the cannon's mouth, replied succinctly, ''Tis said your Ladyship opens your husband's mail.'

Lord Holland's speeches were remarkable for sense and sincerity. He had a well-stocked political memory, and a patient distaste for oratory. He said that the American War had let loose a flood of British eloquence which nothing had since been able to stem. He was stoical under pain, serene under annoyance, and tolerant of everything save injustice. He could forgive Southey his opposition to Catholic Emancipation, having a higher opinion of the poet's heart than of his head. He could derive pleasure from Dr. Samuel Parr's scholarship, though he admitted that there were obstacles to his enjoyment: 'When Parr speaks, nobody can understand what he says, and when he writes, nobody can read his writing.' He could converse smoothly with the historian Hallam, the most fractious and contradictory mortal known to fame. Sydney Smith said that Hallam would leap out of bed for the pleasure of contradicting the night watchman whose duty it was to call the hours. There are men like that. Mark Pattison, scholarly rector of Lincoln, declined to travel on the Continent with Walter Pater, scholarly fellow of Brasenose. 'Pater,' he said, 'would say that the steamboat was not a steamboat, and that Calais was not Calais.'

The company at Holland House was varied; but no one came empty-witted to the board. Palmerston with his rough and ready humour; Brougham with his impish effrontery and his rasping tongue; Melbourne, who spoke rarely and to the point; and Lord Dudley, famed for his repartees, made up a part of that distinguished group. It was long remembered that when a Viennese lady said to Lord Dudley that Londoners spoke French badly, he was kind enough to supply an explanation. 'You see, Madame,' he said, 'we have not enjoyed the advantage of having the French twice in our capital.'

Greville gives a good account of coming late to dinner, and slipping into a vacant chair between Sir George Robinson and a stranger — 'a common-looking man in black.' The table talk turned on early and late education. The man in black casually remarked that Alfieri was ignorant of every art save that of driving until he was twenty-five years old. It then drifted to religious leaders in general and to Saint Ignatius in particular. The man in black supplied some interesting information concerning the wound received by Loyola at the siege of Pampeluna. After that there was a discussion of the law of primogeniture. The man in black told what happened when a Roman died intestate. At this point Greville whispered to Robinson, 'Who is he?' And Robinson whispered back, 'That? Oh, that's Macaulay.'

If Lady Holland was petulantly impatient of Macaulay's erudition, she was none the less alive to the distinction of having him as a guest; and she took it in very bad part when he went to India. Lord Holland, irritated for once beyond his endurance by her egotism, said sharply: 'A man of thirty-four is accorded his first honours, and given his first real income. And you expect him to sacrifice both for the pleasure of dining with you.'

Gifford used to say he wished he could organize a Tory Holland House, to counteract the great Whig stronghold. He knew the value of a non-official council-chamber where the few matured plans, and the many cemented friendships; where party measures were intelligently discussed, and party hopes saved from extinction. He knew also that such considerations alone would never have brought together eminent Whigs who had a natural human distaste for being bored. They came because the dinners were excellent, and the talk was good and gay. Of Sydney Smith it was said that London was his spiritual home, and Holland House was its sanctuary. Lord Holland loved a jest, and being a man to whom any form of excess was profoundly distasteful, he became in time a past-master of understatement. When he said of George the Third that 'his virtues were not of an engaging, nor his endowments of a dazzling character,' it was felt that Wellington could have done no better.

Lady Holland's profoundly sentimental admiration for Napoleon bordered on the ludicrous. Her husband, who felt a noble sympathy for the fall of a great man, and who resented the petty tyrannies to which he was subjected at St. Helena, had hoped that an asylum might be offered him in England; but he ruefully admitted that if there were many Englishwomen who shared his wife's sensibilities, this asylum might have been turned into a shrine. St. Helena being peacefully remote, Lady Holland contented herself with sending books for the exile to read, and delicacies for his table, which, like every other department of his household, was badly supplied. We know that in his last illness and shortly before

146

his death, Napoleon asked for '*les pruneaux de Madame Holland*'; but what many do not know is that the lady's kindness in sending her gifts was equalled by the astuteness with which she made sure of his receiving them. She had, in common with all her friends, a detestation of Sir Hudson Lowe; but she wrote him civil letters, giving him the bits of news that an Englishman remote from London would be glad to hear, and keeping ever in mind that it was through him she might have access to his prisoner. She had known Napoleon at Malmaison in 1802, and she had written to him at Elba. The gold snuff box, ornamented with a cameo, which he bequeathed to her, and which had been the gift of Pope Pius the Sixth, created undue excitement in London. Lord Carlisle wrote a poem, eight stanzas long, begging that the legacy might be refused.

> Lady, reject the gift! Beneath its lid
> Discord and Slaughter and relentless War,
> With every plague to wretched Man lie hid,
> Let not these loose to range the World afar.

This was Pandora's box with a vengeance. Lord Carlisle's verses were published in the *Annual Register*, to which they were well suited; and Byron besought his friend to pay no attention to their warning:

> Lady, accept the box a hero wore,
> In spite of all this elegiac stuff;
> Let not eight stanzas written by a bore
> Prevent your Ladyship from taking snuff.

Lady Holland did not take snuff, and Napoleon did not 'wear' his snuff-box. Otherwise Byron scored.

As the years sped by, the sin which Lady Holland had com-

mitted 'early in life with Methuselah and Enoch' was forgotten. We have Lady Granville's word for it that by 1825
'the most strict, undivorced, and unimpeachable duchesses'
frequented her entertainments. She was firmly entrenched,
she knew her own strength, and she could afford to laugh at
the ill-natured absurdities with which Lady Caroline Lamb
sought to hold her up to ridicule in 'Glenarvon.' What had
she to fear from that bright, broken creature who had not
even known how to make an ally of her influential and profoundly patient husband! Lady Holland had never lacked
allies. She made clear her point of view to Moore when that
poet brought her Byron's 'Memoranda' to read. 'What
people say of me,' she observed, 'gives me no uneasiness. I
know perfectly well my position in the world, and I know
what can be said. As long as the few friends that I am sure
of speak kindly of me (and I would not believe the contrary
if I saw it in black and white), all that the rest of the world
thinks and says is a matter of indifference.'

So spoke the woman who loved her friends, and who died
in part with their deaths. She had the memory of brave
days and of gay nights to sustain her spirit. Her loyalty to her
husband's party was unfaltering. Four toasts were drunk at
the Fox Club to the memory of four great Whigs: Charles
James Fox, Earl Grey, Lord Holland, and Lord John Russell.

> Men are not measured by their wisdom, for none are
> wholly wise; but by their love of justice, which is common
> to all.

VIII

THE PRICE OF LAUGHTER

Be it far from thee to move laughter; for that habit is a slippery descent into vulgarity, and always relaxes the respect of thy friends.

EPICTETUS

VIII

THE PRICE OF LAUGHTER

WHEN Mr. Stephen Leacock alluded casually to Pope Gregory's famous and charming words anent the captive English children, '*Non Angli sed Angeli*,' as one of the oldest puns extant, the comment came as something of a shock. Of course it is a pun, and a very good one. As such it was duly appreciated by a jester like Mr. Leacock. But its note of profound and prophetic sympathy has done more than its wit to keep it alive for thirteen hundred years. No stranger can look for the first time at the amazing beauty of the fair-haired English children without calling it to mind.

The pun has never lacked champions. Charles Lamb said that it was as perfect in its way as a sonnet. But the fact that its perpetrators are always on the defensive shows where it stands in the order of humorous things. George Meredith was of the opinion that 'a sense of the Comic is much blunted by habits of punning and of using humouristic phrases'; but Meredith was always insistently intellectual. He liked Sydney Smith's type of wit, which George Ticknor called 'logic in masquerade.' Sydney did not despise a pun, but he played with ideas rather than with words. When the canons of St. Paul's were discussing the desirability of a wooden pavement around the church, he said to them encouragingly:

'Come, gentlemen, lay your heads together and the thing is done!' A caustic jest which required — as all good jests should — a trickle of thought for its appreciation.

In the last year of the eighteenth century there was born in London the champion punster of England, and, if of England, certainly of the world. His name was Thomas Hood, and he was the son of a bookseller in very moderate circumstances. Blessed with an active spirit, and cursed with a delicate constitution, he was sent when a schoolboy to his mother's relatives in Scotland, to 'the bracing breezes of the north,' warranted to kill or cure. In Hood's case they did neither. He survived the ordeal, but remained physically feeble. After three years at Dundee, where he lived with a kind Scotchwoman who had a seafaring husband, 'as good as dead,' he returned to England, able to do more things badly than most lads of eighteen. He played chess better than he played the flute, and he engraved better than he drew. Indeed it was as an engraver that he meditated earning his bread (his mother was a sister of the skilled workman, Sands), but there were two obstacles in his path: his eyesight was not strong enough for such close work, and he had an overwhelming desire to scribble.

Scribbling came as easy to him as punning. Loose and jagged rhymes flowed from his pen. His early letters were essays; humorous, long-drawn essays that his relatives seem to have liked and read. They could not help liking him. Everybody that met him did. 'A silentish young man,' wrote Lamb to Coleridge, the downcast delicacy of his face redeemed from weakness by a large strong masculine nose. He did not look like the kind of a man to write 'Faithless Sally Brown' and 'Faithless Nelly Gray'; and he wasn't. A misfit in letters, he kept on the wrong track until he died. He had — or he thought he had — no choice.

Yet strokes of pure luck were constantly coming his way. When he was twenty-two, he was given employment as assistant sub-editor of the *London Magazine*, which during its brief and brilliant life contributed to English letters a volume of prose and verse that is our inheritance today. Hood's work was humble, the 'Lion's Mouth,' which he edited, being made up of notices to correspondents, which were for the most part needlessly facetious. But he published in the magazine the tragic 'Lycus the Centaur' and the song 'Fair Inez,' which is more charming than it has any right to be, and so is beloved by poets who understand such things better than the rest of the world. He met intimately Lamb, and Hazlitt, and De Quincey, and, nearest of all, John Hamilton Reynolds, who became his collaborator, his brother-in-law, and, for some years at least, his firm and loving friend.

The book which Hood and Reynolds wrote together had the misfortune to be successful. It was entitled 'Odes and Addresses to Great People,' and was described by Coleridge as 'a little, thin, mean-looking sort of a foolscap sub-octavo of poems, printed on outsides.' Coleridge thought — being a blunderer — that it was the work of Lamb, who was not keenly gratified by his friend's felicitations, and who seized the opportunity to express his views on punning. 'A pun is a thing of too much consequence to be thrown in as a make-weight. It limps ashamed in the retinue of humour; it knows it should have an establishment of its own. Read one of the addresses over, and miss the puns, and it shall be quite as good and better than when you discover 'em.'

Sodden with puns, the 'Odes and Addresses' pleased the public and sold briskly. It also drew from two friends words of counsel which its author would have been well advised to heed. Bryan Waller Procter (Barry Cornwall) expressed a shrewd regret that Hood, who had a real poetic gift, should assume the barren task of 'cracking the shells of jokes which have not always a kernel.' Allan Cunningham wrote him a letter, wise, tolerant, and kind. He acknowledged that a smile had a higher market value than a sigh; but he reminded his friend that he had already done better work than the 'Addresses,' and that he had qualities which must be lost in the perpetual effort of fun-making. There is a tone of genuine regret in his admission that he knows his words will be fruitless. 'Ilka man wears his ain belt his ain gait.'

That his words *were* fruitless was due to a simple circumstance. Hood had been sanguine enough to marry Jane Reynolds, and an income seemed for the nonce more important than a reputation. The 'Addresses' had set a fashion, and established a trade. The jester followed them up with the two series of 'Whims and Oddities,' which he illustrated with drawings of his own. These drawings were in the nature of puns. Their creator was at no time an artist; but he could make his point plain, which was all the public asked. When he wrote 'Oh, listen to my tail of woe,' and illustrated the line with a picture of a puppy with a kettle tied to its poor little tail, everybody saw what he meant. Many things could be funnier than these illustrations, but nothing could be easier to grasp. As for the ballads, 'Faithless Sally Brown' and 'Faithless Nelly Gray,' they must have amused somebody, for they were stolen and hawked about the

streets by ballad mongers who paid nothing to their author.
Hood was always the sport of thieves and beggars. 'Fair
Inez' was ruthlessly snatched from the *London Magazine*,
and reprinted in the tuppeny-hapenny *Literary Magnet*,
without so much as the writer's name, or a word of acknow-
ledgement.

The last years of George the Fourth were destitute of distinction. Hood knew what men of letters there were to be
known; but his acquaintances were for the most part people
who, as Lamb ruefully admitted, encouraged one another
in mediocrity. He belonged to a 'private literary society,'
with a name that 'began in Greek and ended in England';
and he noted with respect the eminence of Miss Hannah
Lawrance, who wrote the 'Historical Memoirs of the Queens
of England,' ahead of Miss Strickland, and the 'History of
Woman in England.' He was greatly harassed to contribute
to ladies' albums, and he was, like Lamb, helpless under
assault. The age was as predatory as our own when it came
to stealing time. It is true that teachers did not then spur
their pupils on to attack harmless writers, demanding
'personal letters' which could be proudly exhibited to a
class. But young women needed no such urging. Their
instinct told them that it was their feminine privilege to
make unreasonable demands. One such marauder, a Miss
Emma Roberts, who was about to sail for India, considered
that this not unusual circumstance justified her in asking
Hood for an original sketch to paste in her album. She was
stimulated to do this 'by the hope of being the only person
who on the banks of the Ganges can boast of possessing a
souvenir from the gentleman to whom the laughter-loving
portion of the community are indebted for so much delight,

and in whose works all those who dwell in every civilized quarter of the globe take so lively an interest.'

Hood, susceptible to flattery, sent this shameless young person, not only the drawing she demanded, but some original and humorous verses entitled 'Lines addressed to Miss Roberts on her Departure to India.' It was so easy for him to do things of this sort; and a busy idleness — the kind called into being by a practical joke — was the thing he loved best on earth. He went to infinite trouble to write Lamb a letter 'on coarse paper and in ragged English,' which purported to come from an aged mendicant, thanking him for the good will manifested in his 'Complaint of the Decay of Beggars.' He took even greater pains to copy Lamb's style (he was at all times an excellent mimic) in an effusion called 'The Widow,' which appeared in 'that accursed annual,' *The Gem,* and was accepted unhesitatingly as 'Elia's' work.

It was in *The Gem* that Hood published during his brief year of editorship his highly dramatic poem, 'The Dream of Eugene Aram,' which will be reprinted in anthologies, and reread by boys and girls, for endless years to come. They will readily forgive (for youth does not balk at trifles) the unpardonable lines, 'My gentle lad,' and 'My gentle boy,' which harrow the souls of adults. It is possible to believe that a murderer who has mistaken his vocation may suffer fierce pangs of remorse. It is possible to believe that he may seek relief for the torment of his soul by telling his miserable tale. But it is not possible to believe that any English usher in any English school ever addressed any English schoolboy as 'my gentle lad.' The thing is incredible.

If Hood turned to the *Comic Annual* as a regrettable but

sure source of income, it was not until he had experienced the difficulty of living without it. His serious poems like 'Hero and Leander' and 'The Plea of the Midsummer Fairies' attracted little notice. They were not good narratives, and they lacked the vein of obvious sentiment which the British public loved. A poem called 'The Pleasures of Hope' or 'The Pleasures of Memory' invited serious attention; but midsummer fairies had no business to plead for a hundred and twenty-six stanzas. Brevity would have become them, but Hood did not know how to be brief. He forgot that it was easier for him to write than it was for other men to read. He forgot that it was not a reading age. Lamb had won for himself a definite and very desirable place in letters, yet no second edition of 'Elia' was published during his lifetime. Well it was for him that a desk in the India House called for his daily attendance, and assured him his daily bread.

On the strength of the *Comic Annual* sales, Hood, who had a genius for making himself uncomfortable, rented the Lake House at Wanstead. An engraving of this residence survives, and it looks more like a mortuary chapel than a home. It was a nice, low-lying, damp, secluded property, with thirty acres for which he had no use, a lake into which friends upset him as a joke (he was a delicate man with a tendency to rheumatic fever), and a salon with painted walls pierced by a large rat hole. Altogether a pompous little structure, destitute of comfort or convenience. We are told that Hood liked to shoot sparrows and rabbits and cats, a displeasing trait which merited not only rat holes but rats. From the Lake House he launched his only novel, 'Tylney Hall,' which failed signally, although young Charles Dickens thought it clever, and Lamb gave it something akin to praise. 'I have been infinitely amused by "Tylney Hall",' he wrote to the author. "Tis a medley without confusion of farce, melodrama, pantomime, comedy, tragedy, punchery and what not? If not the best sort of novel, the best of its sort, as how could it fail, being the only one?'

If Hood was unlucky in his choice of a home, Lamb had no better fortune. His melancholy migrations had begun, and his back was turned upon the only spot in the world where he could hope for content. By night he dreamed of London, and by day he stared disconsolate at the pottering decencies of Enfield. There Hood paid a long-promised visit, and found his friend 'in a bald-looking yellowish house with a bit of a garden, and a wasp's nest convenient, for one stung my pony as it stood at the door.' That was all. Had Lamb abandoned London, 'the moving picture of Fleet Street,' the 'sweet shady side of Pall Mall,' for the greater convenience of a wasp's nest?

Hood was about to do worse. Five years of Wanstead, Comic Annuals, and quarrels with his publishers (Hood's quarrels with his publishers were lifelong) had left him bankrupt, and might have left him bedridden, could he have afforded the luxury of lying in bed. Incurably honest and incurably hopeful, he surrendered all he had to his creditors, left his wife and the Wanstead baby under the kind care of Dr. William Elliott, and departed for Germany, where he fancied himself living the simple life, and working with a carefree mind. The fact that neither he nor Mrs. Hood spoke a word of German did not seem to him a deterrent. The difficulty of editing an annual in England when he was living on the Continent did not even occur to him.

Coblentz was his chosen city, and there his family joined him rather sooner than was expected or convenient.

On the whole, the experiment turned out as well as could have been expected — that is to say no worse than was inevitable. The climate of Coblentz disagreed with Hood; the food sickened him. An immense detestation of Germany and of all things German filled his heart. Especially he hated the Rhine. That admirably picturesque river which so many of his countrymen crossed the channel to see became his *bête noire*; and to escape it he fled to Ostend, where the sea soothed him, and where the greater regularity of the mails enabled him to do his work. Accustomed to turn his discomfitures to good account, he promptly published 'Up the Rhine,' which his countrymen considered humorous, and which in consequence enabled him to return to England, and to forget that there was a German river, or a German castle, or a German student, 'dressed like Macready's William Tell,' in the world.

This was in 1840. Strange things had happened in England while Hood was battling with Coblentz and the German tongue. A merry star danced on the horizon. Sam Weller had made his bow to British readers, who had taken him gratefully to their hearts. 'Oliver Twist' and 'Nicholas Nickleby' had followed swiftly and irresistibly. Life had grown gayer with their advent. There was a well-founded conviction that a man who did not laugh at Mrs. Nickleby would never laugh at anything on earth. Moreover, if he were more readily moved to pity and to anger than to laughter, there was a deep resentment in the young novelist's heart which could amply feed his flame. On this point, Hood, sick, worn, and disheartened, was in perfect accord with Dickens. He, too, had hated all his life the careless in-justice of time-honoured British institutions. He had warm praise for 'Oliver Twist,' for its vigour, its realism, the bitter lesson that it taught. But it did not occur to him for a moment that the Dodger and Charley Bates were amusing companions.

There were but a few more years left to Hood, but in them he was to do his most famous work. The death of Theodore Hook had deprived the *New Monthly Magazine* of an editor, and the post was offered to Hood with a salary of three hundred pounds — little enough, Heaven knows, but a sure thing for so long as he could keep from quarrelling with his publishers. By a miracle of grace, he did abstain for nearly three years. Then the inevitable happened; but not before he had published in the *New Monthly* 'Miss Kilmansegg and her Precious Leg,' pronounced his masterpiece by excellent critics who have not read it all. When the 'all' consists of three hundred and forty-one brilliant and satirical stanzas that came reeling off Hood's pen as though he could not stop them, it is easier to praise than to read. It was the last step, never the first, that cost this prodigal poet his supreme effort.

When Southey died in 1843, Hood wrote to Sir Charles Dilke suggesting himself as a successor to the laureate. The honour was accorded to Wordsworth; but it does sometimes happen that a thing is to be had for the seeking. Mr. E. F. Benson is responsible for the story that Lord Salisbury, on being asked why he had appointed Mr. Alfred Austin to the laureateship, answered simply: 'So far as I can remember, no one else applied for the post.'

In 1841 the pursuit of laughter had received a fresh im-

petus in England. *Punch* made its triumphant appearance.
Destined to play an important rôle in its country's welfare,
its cartoons have told history better than historians have
told it; and its unconquerable jests have inspirited men's
hearts in long periods of disaster. It aimed at reproducing
exactly the aspects of social and political life at which it
mocked; and for nearly a hundred years it has been Britain's
chronicler. If it occasionally blundered (*vide* 'The Yarn of
the Nancy Bell'), who, or what, is infallible? Its early contributors embraced most of the humorous talent in England,
and Hood's name is not to be found among them. The
public was sickening of puns, and the great punster could
not shake off the habit of a lifetime. Charles Cowden Clarke
describes him at this time as a man whose 'worn pallid look
strangely belied the effect of jocularity and high spirits conveyed in his writings. He punned incessantly, but lan-
guidly, almost as if he were unable to think in any other
fashion than in a play upon words.'

What had this representative of the outworn to give to
the new generation of laughter-lovers? Nothing to laugh at,
perhaps, but assuredly something to listen to. The Christmas
of 1843 was approaching when *Punch* received a poem which
seemed eminently unfitted for its cheerful pages, but which
its editor, Mr. Mark Lemon, was reluctant to let go. He was
the kind of editor to whom a strong impulse counted for
more than reasoning; and so in the Christmas number, amid
the usual jumble of jokes and sentiment, of plum-puddings
and mistletoe, there appeared some unsigned, unillustrated
verses entitled 'The Song of the Shirt.'

The immediate result was to treble the sale of the Christmas *Punch*. The far-reaching effect was to arouse a passion

of pity for the underpaid. The time was ripe for this pity to find expression, for the poor-laws and the courts were pitilessly cruel. The flame of indignation that burned in Hood's heart had dictated his words, strong simple words that could not be misunderstood. 'The Song of the Shirt' was printed on cheap handkerchiefs, pinned on ballad boards, chanted like a rude dirge by men, women, and children on the streets. The singers reminded one another that a needle-woman had been charged at the Lambeth police court with pawning articles of clothing belonging to her employer. She had been making trousers for seven pence a pair, and the utmost she could earn was seven shillings a week. This was considered as 'a good living for a woman who had herself and two young children to support.'

The homeliness of Hood's verses gave them their unrivalled success. By their side other heartfelt appeals seemed studied and artificial. 'The Lady's Dream' was but a shadow, and Mrs. Browning's tragic 'Cry of the Children' was difficult of approach. Plain people were perplexed when they read:

> How long, O cruel nation,
> Will you stand, to move the world, on a child's heart,
> Stifle down with a mailèd heel its palpitation,
> And tread onward to your throne amid the mart?'

But they knew as well as the wisest what Hood meant when he wrote:

> O men with sisters dear,
> O men with mothers and wives,
> It is not linen you're wearing out,
> But human creatures' lives.

and they felt what he felt in his sick, scornful heart:

> It's oh, to be a slave
> Along with the barbarous Turk,
> Where woman has never a soul to save,
> If this be Christian work.

There is no mistaking the sincerity and the profound pity that prompted these lines. If Hood failed to renew their inspiration in 'The Lay of the Labourer,' he put himself on record as a champion of the oppressed when he protested against the sentence passed upon Gifford White, a young farmhand of Bluntisham. This lad of eighteen had written a letter threatening incendiarism if he were given no chance to work; for which offence (a sinister one) he was tried at the Huntingdon Assizes, and sentenced to transportation for life. Hood had troubles of his own, and his torch was burning low; but he spared time and strength to plead against a pitiless judgment inspired by the most cruel of all emotions, fear. 'Were I a Bluntisham farmer,' he wrote, 'I could not sleep soundly, and know that for my sake a son of the same soil had been rooted out like a common weed, and sent a banished man, not for a little while, or for a long while, but for ever.'

It is typical of Hood's career that with only one more year to live he should have started a new monthly magazine. Had he been on his deathbed, this would have seemed to him an eminently fitting way of spending his last hours. *Hood's Magazine* the newcomer was called, and the name was well bestowed; for although it had a strong corps of contributors, more than half of the first issue was the work of his own pen. That amazing *tour de force*, 'The Haunted

House,' must have filled many pages, and chilled many hearts. It is long, but its undue length makes it the more masterly. It is monotonous, but its monotony is intentional and oppressive. How could any poet have maintained unbroken that melancholy cadence, that close characterization, which leaves nothing unobserved from the apple rotting on the cankered tree to the spider that

> up its slender thread
> Ran with a nimble terror!

An accomplished scholar, the Reverend G. P. A. Longmore, translated 'The Haunted House' into Latin; and the beat of that measured tongue must have rendered with fidelity the sombre, steadfast burden of the poem.

In the second number of *Hood's Magazine* appeared 'The Bridge of Sighs.' Then the editor's contributions stopped abruptly because he was dying. Peel had persuaded Queen Victoria that a pension of one hundred pounds would be fittingly bestowed upon him, and that, as he could not possibly live to enjoy it, such a benefaction would be a mockery unless it were continued to his widow. So many offers of aid had poured in upon Devonshire Lodge that, after the poet's death, his admirers were emboldened to open a 'Memorial Fund' for his family. Nearly fourteen hundred pounds were subscribed, the subscribers ranging all the way from Peel, who sent fifty pounds, to 'a few journeymen tailors' who managed to raise a half-crown for the widow of the man who had been their friend. Seven years later another subscription was set on foot for the monument in Kensal Green Cemetery, and for this the money was quickly raised. So far as men like to give at all, they like to give to monuments, which yield solid and substantial proofs of liberality. Hood's certainly did. There is a tall shaft and a bust of the writer. There is a comic mask to show that he was a humourist, and a lyre to show that he was a poet. There is a wreath of bay leaves, and what appears to be a wreath of ivy buds. There is also on the lower step of the pedestal a globe which doubtless has its significance, and above them all is the line: 'He sang the Song of the Shirt.'

Mrs. Browning told Frederick Locker that she preferred Hood's poetry to Gray's, adding serenely: 'But then I do not care very much for Gray.' The remark is of interest because it furnishes a key to Mrs. Browning's verse. She rejected the only English poet who never wrote a line too much in favour of the poet who never did anything else, save in a few minor poems. These poems have endeared him to all editors and readers of anthologies. Garnett pronounced 'The Song of the Shirt' and 'The Bridge of Sighs' to be true *volkslieder* of the nineteenth century. If the latter poem shows some concessions to sentiment:

Young and so fair!

both embody the compassion which was the animating motive of Hood's work, and both stand alone in the potency of their appeal.

Other brief poems are familiar and beloved. 'I Remember, I Remember' is a true anthology lyric, always at hand and always welcome. No matter how little a man has made of his life, he is disposed to grow sentimental over the spot where life began, and to be a trifle sorry for the hospital-born babies of today who can lay no claim to a decently individual birthplace. The 'Ode to Autumn,' the lilting song, 'A lake and a fairy boat,' and 'Fair Inez' are sure of readers. 'The witty and tender Hood,' said Landor, who did not fling his praises about, and whose words have in them a note of deep and serious regard.

Wit is a thing capable of proof. 'If you tell me you are witty,' observed Augustine Birrell, 'I must trouble you to make a joke.' Hood made them by the thousand, but they are savourless and spiritless today. The need of jesting for a livelihood, a need he deliberately assumed, made him 'poor Hood' to all his friends, who ceased laughing at his drolleries long before he had ceased producing them. 'Hood's marvellous facility for words,' says Stephen Leacock, 'helped to drive the pun to death at the hands of an exhausted public.' One would like to think so; but *Punch* was as full of puns as a pincushion is full of pins for years after Hood died; and À Beckett's 'Comic Histories' of England and of Rome are so congested with puns that only the flawless fun of John Leech's pictures can carry the reader over them. Nevertheless, there was a change in the fashion of jesting about this time, and for such a change Hood was in a measure responsible. He had punned unceasingly for twenty-five years, and the public was sated if not exhausted. Moreover his extraordinary skill in playing with words made other punsters seem unduly painstaking. His eminence was everywhere acknowledged. The clever draftsman, Alfred Forrester, paid him this tribute in a quatrain which was very much to the taste of the time:

Wits may now lay aside their pens,
        Their sallies being no good;
Till thou art dead they cannot hope
        To — urn a lively Hood.

It is like a well-fitted piece of joiner's work, and about as amusing. But it must have delighted Hood as a masterstroke of his own art executed in his honour. The pursuit of laughter was his life's work. What it cost him and what it cost his readers we know only by a sense of loss when we recognize the quality of a few stray poems. His complete works, published after his death, filled eleven volumes. What is left to us today is little enough, but it has the attribute of permanence.

IX

THE TWENTIETH CENTURY

C'est une étrange entreprise — celle de faire rire les honnêtes gens.

MOLIÈRE

IX

THE TWENTIETH CENTURY

In the winter of 1877 Mr. George Meredith gave in London a lecture on 'Comedy and the Uses of the Comic Spirit.' The paper appeared subsequently in the *New Quarterly*; and twenty years later was republished by Scribners in a remarkably neat little volume. Its purport is to show that while the 'big round laugh' of an earlier generation (the laugh of the Middle Ages which the Church hushed down) is silenced for ever, its place has been taken by the 'finely tempered smile' which recognizes and welcomes the comic spirit. Sensitiveness to this spirit the author considers a step in the civilization of the world.

All that Mr. Meredith set forth in this address has been condensed by Santayana into one brief and pregnant sentence: 'Everything in life is lyrical in its ideal, tragic in its fate, and comic in its existence.' But nowhere does the philosopher observe any recognition of these attributes on the part of humanity. The lyric in life is observed by a few men with cultivated minds and sensitive souls; the tragic is felt, but not understood; the comic puzzles and affronts. Its essence is the discovery and rejection of the absurd which blocks the advancement of the world. People who cannot recognize a palpable absurdity are very much in the way of civilization. Meredith was of the opinion that the Germans, though merry and full of fun, lacked the comic sense, and that one reason for this national loss was their reluctance to sharpen and enjoy the intelligence of their women.

Eighteen years after this observation, the Emperor Wilhelm the Second wrote to Queen Victoria, whom he had honoured with a visit which neither of them had enjoyed, saying he hoped that she would stop the publication of *Punch*. He would have hoped it far more ardently could he have foreseen the part that this great weekly would play in the World War; but how could a widely informed man, well past his youth, have been guilty of such a bêtise? He knew too much about England and too much about the Queen to have made it seem possible. Victoria had no lasting quarrel with *Punch*; but there were books published in her day (the 'Greville Memoirs,' for example) which she would have been glad to suppress had that been one of her prerogatives. Her grandson's offhand request must have shown her once and for all the danger that lies in an inability to apprehend the absurd.

Years later, when the war was on, when England was struggling in deep waters, and the United States was facing every day new problems and emergencies, Walter Page, our representative in London, and probably the most overworked man in Christendom, received a delegation of six American clergymen who had passed a resolution 'urging our Ambassador to telegraph our beloved and peace-loving President to stop this awful war.' 'And they came,' wrote Page, 'with simple solemnity to present this resolution. Lord save us, what a world!'

Examples might be multiplied. It is a pity that Meredith gave so much space in his brief pages to the comedy of the stage, and so little to the comedy of life. He thought that an acquaintance with stagecraft might sharpen men's wits, and he could not foresee a day when the cinema would hustle the drama into a corner, and present a form of entertainment to which the comic sense offers no avenue of approach. Laughter has always been open to perversion. It reaches its lowest level in the cinema, which appeals deliberately to crude emotions and to mental immaturity, which seeks above all things to make no trouble for itself, and which in its endlessly repeated 'comics' has never ventured to hold up to ridicule those dangerous absurdities which have destroyed the prosperity and lowered the pride of the nation. 'The United States,' says Mr. Elmer Davis, 'has as good a government as the majority of voters are willing to tolerate.' So caustic a jest should provoke something beyond the meaningless laugh with which men admit an evil that they do not intend to remedy.

Americans have always believed themselves to be a humorous people. The Declaration of Independence was ushered into the world with as good a witticism from as accomplished a wit as ever history has recorded. The mental maturity of our early statesmen, compared to whom we now seem a nation of youths, enabled them to cultivate a comic sense, and pioneer conditions are favourable to fun. It cannot be said that American humour moved along Franklin's lines. Its texture was of a simpler sort, woven out of the most incongruous elements of life, and fitted to the needs of clear-eyed, uneducated men. Franklin was a scholar — self-taught, but none the less scholarly. Let him read Swift or Molière if he wanted to be amused. A single century separated him from Abraham Lincoln, who extracted from Artemus Ward the laughter he coveted and required. It may be that the erratic spelling of this American humourist represented to Lincoln's mind a freedom from schooling which lent emphasis to the homely sapience of the text. 'What the pun was to England,' says Mr. Leacock, 'bad spelling was to America. A whole generation of Artemus Wards traded on bad spelling. In the end they killed it as dead as the dead pun in England.'

More dead, we trust, if there are degrees of dissolution. The only interest we take in this cold-blooded murder of orthography is to wonder how it was done. Did its perpetrators spell phonetically without pausing to think what variations might ensue; or did they spell as they had been taught to spell, and then readjust the letters for the press? It sounds laborious and profitless, but it was dear to American hearts. Artemus Ward and Josh Billings and Bill Nye all misspelled, but they did not misspell alike. The Biglow Papers were misspelled, but only so far as a presumably Yankee dialect would permit. The nineteenth century wanted to laugh as much as did any of its predecessors. The twentieth century seems to have lost this desire. How much it is amused by Gertrude Stein, and how much it reveres her as something too deep for understanding, it would be hard to say.

The early death of Artemus Ward deprived his country of a man who might have travelled far. He had the upbringing which secured a fairly good knowledge of humanity, and he saw things from a humorous angle. The stories that are told about him are better than the stories he told, because he worked his jokes — the Mormon joke for instance — to death. Polygamy was something exquisitely amusing to Americans. It admitted the exaggeration which was our favourite substitute for wit. A man with three wives was as dull as a man with one; but a man with thirty wives might be made entertaining for a time. Ward's favourite anecdote of a young friend who had run away with a boarding-school was so delightfully new to London that his audience failed to grasp its point.

Personally he must have been a singularly amusing companion. Humour bubbling up in a man's daily speech is very different from humour embalmed in books and lectures. 'Artemus the delicious,' Charles Reade called him, and the words had meaning. When a theatrical manager in San Francisco wired him, 'What will you take for forty nights in California?' Ward wired back: 'Brandy and water.' If not actually witty, that telegram had a quality which ensured for its recipient the 'big round laugh' so rapidly disappearing from the world. To Ward has been ascribed a real witticism which he may have said, though it has other claimants: 'The trouble with Napoleon was that he tried to do too much, and did it.' He is also one of the men — and there are very few — who have been undeniably humorous on their deathbeds. He was nearing the end when he refused to take some physic which the doctor thought might give him relief. 'Do take it,' urged the playwright, Tom Robertson, 'for my sake. There is nothing I would not do for yours.'

'Is that true?' murmured the dying man.

'As gospel,' said Robertson.

'Then,' said Ward, 'you take it' — and scored.

Forty thousand copies of Ward's funny stories were sold in the United States. Those were not days when volumes came tumbling in torrents from the press — masterpieces, best-sellers, prize-winners, books of the month, all of them hailed as forerunners of a new era, all of them clamoured for at public libraries, all of them discussed by women's clubs and by college freshmen, all of them enjoying deep regard until pushed roughly out of the way by the next torrent, and consigned to oblivion. In 1850 our country had not yet been dipped in ink, and forty thousand books, slim little volumes most of them, was considered a marvellous sale for a man who died at thirty-three. There was no such passionate pursuit of laughter until Mark Twain's star shone on the horizon.

Not that Americans were ungrateful to their lesser lights. They bought and read Josh Billings and Bill Nye, and misquoted them so continuously that nothing is harder now than to be sure of who said what. Josh Billings was more sensible than jocular. 'If you want tew git a sure krop, and a big yield for the seed, sow wilde oats,' suggests 'Poor Richard.' It would have delighted Franklin's heart, and was probably printed in the 'Farmer's Almanac,' a very profitable publication. 'Misfortunes and twins hardly ever come singly,' is neatly said, but only moderately amusing. Indeed Billings (otherwise Mr. Henry Shaw) was aware of his own shortcomings. 'We have not yet had time,' he said adroitly, 'to boil down our humour, and get the wit out of it.'

Bill Nye, who came along some years later, is, like Artemus Ward, more entertaining to read about than to read. There is something novel and refreshing in his description of his father's farm in Wisconsin, 'a hundred and sixty acres of beautiful ferns and bright young rattlesnakes'; and in his account of his own childhood spent in going to school 'between Indian massacres.' He dealt largely in that exaggeration which has been discredited by sophisticated wits, and which Mrs. Meynell assures us we should resent because it appeals to our credulity. But pioneers delighted in its childishness, which made no appeal whatever to anybody's credulity. The Yankee tourist who said he had observed 'some rising ground' in Switzerland; the Mississippi captain who said he could sail his boat wherever the country was a little damp, did not seek to be believed. All they wanted was to go so far that nobody could go any farther, which is precisely what children aim at in their fantastic lying.

In every phase of early American humour we see the desperate need of our fathers for laughter. Bright young rattlesnakes and Indian massacres — whether the Indians massacred us or we massacred the Indians — were uneasy elements in life. Then there were the Civil War, and the enfranchised Negroes, and the crystal-clear shamelessness of politicians. When Mark Twain came along with a 'Jumping Frog' in his pocket, a harassed public welcomed him with rapture. The Frog, so we are told, 'ran through the newspapers of the country.' It was translated, as a jest, into French, and retranslated into English, to be laughed at anew. By the time it was squeezed dry of laughter its creator was a made man, lecturing successfully in the West, and ready to start on the tour which was to inspire 'Innocents Abroad.'

He had enjoyed the best of training for his life's work.

Able, like Franklin and Walt Whitman, to set type at thirteen, he knocked about the country as a journeyman printer and a river pilot on the Mississippi, earning his bread and seeing the world. The great river was to him a never-ending marvel, changeful, provocative, and perilous. What he did not know about its sixty glorious years of travel and traffic was not worth knowing. His pen name was a river term meaning two fathom deep, a circumstance which gave him infinite delight. In his masterpiece, 'Huckleberry Finn,' and in that ponderous, prolix, and entertaining book, 'Life on the Mississippi,' he tried hard to share his knowledge with his readers. The courage and cheerfulness of his early manhood suffered an eclipse when he took to speculating upon life instead of living it with prodigality. In 1899 he wrote to Mr. Howells: 'I have been reading the morning paper. I do it every day — well knowing that I shall find in it the usual depravities and basenesses and hypocrisies and cruelties that make up civilization, and cause me to put in the rest of the day pleading for the damnation of the human race.'

This is not the language of a humourist, nor, to say truth, of a philosopher. It is not depravity that afflicts the human race so much as a general lack of intelligence. Mr. Howells was too admiring a friend to be critical. He was capable of saying that 'A Connecticut Yankee in King Arthur's Court' was as 'compellingly and independently creative as "Don Quixote."' He probably did not really think so, but he said it, oblivious to the fact that the training of a river pilot, while superb along its own lines, could not be trusted to open a man's mind to the vision of the sixth century — to its cruelty and its holiness, its supreme indifference to comfort, its rapturous visions of beauty. The consideration of

contrasts can always raise a laugh, but it offers no approach
to understanding.

Yet what a glorious time Mark Twain had of it! The
idol of his own country and of England, the recipient of
honours from Oxford, beloved by his friends, and deeply
respected by the public for the courage with which in the
face of misfortune he had upheld his personal integrity,
sure of himself and convinced that his opinions — however
arrived at — were correct, his old age seems like a golden
and red sunset. Yet a year or two before he died he wrote a
fantastic tale called 'The Mysterious Stranger,' which closes
with a diatribe against God that reads like a speech at a
political convention, when a Republican orator gives his
opinion of a Democratic candidate — or vice versa. From
an insane world and from an iniquitous — though non-
existent — Deity the author seeks what relief he can find in
complete negation. He is but a thought — 'a vagrant
thought, a useless thought, a homeless thought, wandering
forlorn among the empty eternities.'

Happily for us and for the memory of Mark Twain,
'Huckleberry Finn' is the kind of thought that survives. It
was said of the ever-famous Keate, master of Eton, that he
understood one truth which Arnold of Rugby never grasped
— that the Almighty had made something between a child
and a man which was a boy. Nobody ever knew this important truth better than did Twain. Huckleberry Finn is
the product of his environment. There could never have
been a great many little boys like him. But he is so much
alive that the man who bade him live had no reasonable
excuse for doubting his own superabundant vitality.

Thirty years separated the jester, Mark Twain, from the

jester, Peter Finley Dunne, otherwise Mr. Dooley. Chicago was growing in Mark Twain's day. It had grown in Mr. Dooley's, and was for him, very properly, the centre of the universe. From his own ward and from his own bar in Archey Road he looked out upon life, and engaged in the proper study of mankind. Those were good days in which to live. Our skirmish with Spain was over, and we talked about it and wrote about it in terms that would have befitted Marathon. Mr. Hennessy is as enthusiastic about our 'histing the flag over the Ph'lippeens' as if he had not just found out that they were islands, and not, as he had previously supposed, canned goods. A sense of well-being permeates Mr. Dooley's pages. The White House cat is named 'Gold Bonds'; mortgages spell security; the price of whisky, 'fifteen cents a slug,' remains immovable in days of peace and war; the 'almighty dollar' has the superb impregnability that once attached itself to Roman citizenship; and devout men breathe a prayer that Providence may remain under the protection of the American flag.

Naturally a philosopher writing in the sunshine differs from a philosopher writing in the shade. Will Rogers essayed a rôle somewhat similar to Mr. Dooley's; but, being a more versatile genius, he wasted his powers of observation. Only now and then did he say a terse word, unqualified and unkind: 'Americans are not worrying over the League of Nations. What they want is some place to park their cars.' Or again when President Roosevelt had chosen his helpmates in office: 'The forgotten man has been found. There's nine of him and one woman in the cabinet.' Mr. Dooley's remarks have less national significance; but they are as sardonic and a good deal more amusing. The conversion

of the Chippeway Indians into 'a cimitry branch iv th'
Young Men's Christian Association' is not unsatisfactory
to him. His disapproval of ghosts is supremely reasonable:
'Whin a man's dead, he ought to make th' best iv a bad job,
an' not be thrapsin' around, lookin' f'r throuble among his
own kind.' His magniloquence in patriotic moments is
sublime: 'I have seen America spread out fr'm th' Atlantic
to th' Pacific, with a branch office iv th' Standard Ile Com-
p'ny in ivry hamlet. I've seen the shackles dropped fr'm th'
slave, so's he cud be lynched in Ohio.' Even his glance at
England is comprehensive: 'Great Britain has ixtinded her
domain until th' sun niver sets on it. No more do th' original
owners iv th' sile, they bein' kept movin' be th' polis.'

Mr. Thomas Masson, one of the brilliant founders and
editors of *Life*, always maintained that Americans lacked a
sense of humour, which was an ungrateful as well as a mistaken thing to say. In his day they supported three flourish-
ing comic weeklies, which were sold on every railway stand,
and read seriously and sadly by every traveller. The sub-
stitution of motors for trains struck a heavy blow at periodical literature. Men in a train dozed tranquilly over their
magazines. Men in motors are like men in the front line of
battle. The question for them is who are to survive.

Mr. Masson claimed for himself the privilege of being
serious in private life. It was as unreasonable, he considered,
to expect a humourist to be always funny as to expect a poet
to be always poetical, or a doctor to be always scientific. Of
course, no one would tolerate the poet or the doctor, while
everybody waits breathlessly for a wit to be witty, or for a
satirist to be satirical, which proves that Mr. Masson was
wrong about his public. He tells us that he was once elected

'by a mysterious political fluke' to be the president of a board of education; and found out afterwards that he owed his honours to a not unnatural desire on the part of the board to be amused. It was hoped that he would enliven the meetings with comments and stories which, being necessarily irrelevant, would divert the members from their educational labours.

Surely this incident is in itself sufficient to prove that Americans have a sense of humour. Such a sense does not mean the possession of humour but the appreciation of it. We want to laugh, even if we have little to laugh at. There is no American Dickens, but our enjoyment of him was as keen as England's. There is no American Shaw, but we have crowded the theatres when his plays were acted. Dickens jeered at us, and Shaw has expressed from time to time his distaste for our qualities; but these verdicts have left us undisturbed. After all, England forgave Mark Twain his far deeper misunderstanding. A friend is a friend, and Santayana — detached from ephemeralities — says that Dickens is 'one of the best friends mankind has ever had.'

He is! If a new generation has discarded him, its loss is a grievous one. Men and women will live out their lives, and never know that in an unread book by an abandoned novelist there is a little girl named Morleena Kenwigs. If they met her but once they would perforce recognize the genius that could devise such a name, that could assemble a few dull letters of the alphabet, and make them unforgettable. Morleena Kenwigs! It is a work of art. Pecksniff is Pecksniff because he had to be. That was his name, waiting for him through the centuries. He would not have been recognizable by any other. But Morleena Kenwigs is a pure invention, and Dickens, having so endowed the child, sketches her lightly for our delectation. Mrs. Kenwigs is busy having her sixth baby, and Morleena, 'as the eldest of the family, and the representative of her mother during her indisposition, had been hustling and slapping the younger Misses Kenwigs without intermission; which conduct brought tears into the eyes of Mr. Kenwigs, and caused him to declare that, in understanding and behaviour, that girl was a woman. "She will be a treasure to her husband," he said. "I think she'll marry above her station, Mr. Lumbey."

'"I shouldn't wonder at all," replied the doctor.'

Ten years after Morleena had slapped her little sisters, and when every man or woman who learned the alphabet made one more reader for Dickens, a critic in the *North American Review* regretted that this popular novelist should have been 'led away from the simplicity of truth by a tricksy spirit of fantastic exaggeration.' It was like saying that he regretted Dickens should have been a humorous instead of a serious writer. The simplicity of truth has a great deal to recommend it, but comedy is not one of its qualifications. Mrs. Nickleby wanders farther and farther from exactness as she unfolds her admirable absurdities. But Mrs. Nickleby in life must have been very dull; and Mrs. Nickleby in the novel is very amusing. Moreover she runs always true to form. Dickens's exaggerations are not like the exaggerations of the Yankee tourist or the Mississippi captain. They are illustrative and satiric, like the exaggeration of Palmerston when he told Delane that he had set the study chimney at Broadlands on fire with Gladstone's resignations.

Mr. Stephen Leacock is of the opinion that it took the

nineteenth century to develop the American grin into the American laugh, and that even now the humour of the American press is strait-jacketed by restrictions. A mocker in our morning paper must be careful at whom he mocks. He must see to it that he does not offend syndicates, or organized labour, or trusts, or socialists, or Jews, or spiritualists, or reformers, or any body of people strong enough to retaliate. He is in the position of the little girl, who, having been reproached with some vehemence for kicking her kind nurse, said despairingly: 'I can't kick Father, and I can't kick Mother, and I can't kick the baby. If I can't kick Nannie, whom *am* I to kick?' Yet kicking, which is a natural outlet for ill-temper, is also the foundation of much fun. It ensures a sufferer for the joke.

As for a grin, it is to us more expressive of enjoyment than is a laugh. An American will grin where a Negro will laugh loudly and without merriment. We are not startled into grinning as we are startled into laughter. We may in our day have laughed at some uproarious caricature of Gillray's or of Nast's which we have never wanted to see again; but who does not remember the grin with which we looked long and lovingly at Phil May's London sketches? The happy successor of John Leech, May surpassed all of *Punch's* draughtsmen in the austerity of his workmanship. The process of elimination has never been carried further than by his unsparing hand. The nearness of the tragic to the comic has never been more clearly conceived. 'Guttersnipes' must last as long as children and poverty last; and as children and poverty contribute loyally to each other's survival, their day is likely to be a long one.

The great caricaturists have been politicians who made

their victims obnoxious by ridiculing them. An acute German who visited London when Gillray was at the height of his fame said truly that England was 'altogeder von libel.' Gillray's first caricature of Lord North was drawn when he was twelve years old, and from that time on he never desisted from his cruel sport. He worked in a sort of frenzy, speeding through a print as though he had not another hour to live. For thirty years England gave his work a never-failing welcome. The crowd around his famous shop on Old Bond Street was so persistent that passers-by took to the gutters. It does not appear that this crowd was easily affronted. It did not want taste or decency. It wanted the supreme exaggeration which is the triumph of the caricature. It wanted the distortion of the human figure which the Greeks so deeply resented. It wanted daring conception, brilliant execution, coarseness, and nastiness. It wanted, and it got, a pursuit of laughter too furious for sanity. Nothing was more inevitable than that madness should intervene, and put a stop to the artist's labours.

Compared to Gillray, Cruikshank (who had a highly comic name) was a gentle creature. His persevering animosity to George the Fourth was ungentle; but at that date it was customary to attack some crowned head, and George lent himself amiably to assault. Louis Philippe, the most caricatured of monarchs, acquired that proud pre-eminence solely because the shape of his head was an irresistible temptation to artists. Cruikshank was a better illustrator than a caricaturist, and a better moralist than either. 'Moral comedies' was the Hogarthian epithet applied to his prints. The sight of two women dangling from the gallows for having passed forged notes of one pound each roused him to such a pitch of anger and grief that a single plate sufficed to awaken popular indignation. *That* crime was stricken off the list of capital offences. It was harder to fight the sodden drunkenness of the day; but Cruikshank accomplished more with the vigorous drawing entitled 'The Bottle' than did all the other temperance workers in England. It cannot be claimed that these prints are humorous, but neither is Gin Lane.

What Gillray was to Britain, Thomas Nast was to the United States, an able politician and an unrelenting caricaturist. He told history as a cartoonist should, clearly and vigorously, but he cared very little whether he told it truly or not. Lincoln said of him that he was the best recruiting sergeant the Administration ever had; Cleveland measured his failing powers, and made all possible use of them; and Theodore Roosevelt sent him, a broken and impoverished old man, to drowse and die as a consul in Ecuador. His great achievement was his fairly successful combat with the Democratic control of New York. The concentrated bitterness of 'The Tammany Tiger Let Loose' did more than any single cartoon had ever done to further this good end. He enriched the political field with its three emblematic animals — the tiger, the donkey, and the elephant; and, while none of them seem especially relevant, they bid fair to roam these gusty pastures for many years to come.

Bernard Shaw declares that he has seen dramatic critics 'rocking with laughter' over his plays. Since he goes out of his way to say this, they must have done so, but the picture does not visualize easily. For years we rocked with laughter over Charlie Chaplin's films. There was no other way of expressing our delight. But if Shaw makes us laugh, he also makes us think. The laugh is incidental, the thought is fundamental. If we are sufficiently educated and sufficiently intelligent to think, our range of humour is wider than if we were less well endowed. We do not have to wonder what Shaw is driving at. We guess, more or less successfully, what he is driving at, and devote our attention to the drive. But the man or woman who has a mature mind does not enjoy elementary fun unless it be — like Charlie Chaplin's — exceptionally amusing, and shot through with moments of emotion. The comic film does not reach the dead level of imbecility which distinguishes the comic strips in our daily press; that would be impossible; but it is without acuteness, and without intelligible purpose. The strolling actors of the Middle Ages were, by comparison, satirists and courageous satirists. Many a time they dared the whipping-post for the sake of a just cause or a popular joke.

In view of this fact, Mr. Leacock might have paused before he pronounced the Middle Ages destitute of humour, and offered, as proof, the fact that the monks never got beyond a Latin epigram or acrostic. They probably had jests of their own, mostly levelled at one another, and repeated as often as the monastery could endure. The humour of communities is apt to run along these lines. But it was not the business of monks to provide laughter for the laity, nor was there any need. What they had to do was to preach soberness of spirit, and the likelihood of being damned. For this they had the example of the Fathers of the Church; of Saint Basil, for example, who frowned upon jesting even while he jested. Summoned before the angry Governor of Pontus who threatened to tear out his liver, Basil rejoined that, as located, it had never given him anything but trouble. His beloved friend and fellow recluse, Saint Gregory of Nazianzus, was a confirmed jester who mocked cheerfully at the austerities they practised; at the hunks of ill-baked bread, at the pot-herbs which were a substitute for food, at Basil, 'hungry and cross' for lack of sustenance. There was greater freedom in the fourth than in the fourteenth century. The heavy battery of medieval jokes which required purging, the ripple of medieval laughter which called for silencing, were yet unheard. Men had set aside the customs and traditions of paganism, and had not grown into Christian customs and traditions. They denied the pagan love of life, and knew nothing of the mounting joy which came with the ages of architecture. They were sobered by past persecutions, beset by present schisms, and instructed by very enlightened scholars.

As for pursuing laughter, and justifying the pursuit, that would have seemed a needless waste of energy to any age but ours. England has striven to laugh since the days of Elizabeth; but she has not been conscious of the effort. The French have contented themselves with pursuing life, open-eyed and unafraid. They have laughed and wept as life has bade them. This clearness of vision has made them supremely intelligent, but it has not made them happy. No one can imagine a French educator proposing, as a superintendent of schools in Chicago proposed a few years ago, that courses in the appreciation of humour should be given in 'all the educational institutes of the country.' That superintendent sincerely believed that laughter should be pursued, and subjected to intensive cultivation. The 'happiness index' of the student who had been told what to laugh at, and when to consider himself amused, would necessarily be higher than the happiness index of the student who had been left to the careless ministrations of nature.

There have always been men who set great store by laughter, but who could neither enjoy it nor help others to its enjoyment. Hazlitt was such a man. He had been brought up too seriously, had read sermons when he was too young, had been unwise in love, unlucky in marriage, and unduly eccentric in the matter of eating and drinking. This last error was disastrous. 'There remains to us,' says the wise Santayana, 'eating and drinking, relished, not bestially, but humanly and jovially as the sane and exhilarating basis for everything else.'

Hazlitt was a humourist so far as acute intelligence and study could make one. He analyzed humour until his readers doubted its existence. He resolved laughter into its component parts, and sighed over the silence that ensued. He held Hudibras to be England's masterpiece of wit, and so did Charles the Second. He thought Punch and Judy shows irresistibly funny, and so did George the Third. He longed perpetually for the comedies of the Restoration, and so did Charles Lamb. But Charles the Second died before England's keenest wits were born. George the Third was not precisely the intellectual ally that Hazlitt would have chosen. Charles Lamb, though conscious of the dulness that enveloped him, found in it material for the most permanently humorous letters that ever an Englishman wrote.

There were many things that Lamb disliked. According to Mr. Blunden, there were far too many. 'Churches, Goethe, the Lake District, philosophy, punctuality, Shelley's voice, sanity, Scots, Jews, and schoolmasters.' He could not have escaped them all, and he did not try, because he never expected the circumstances of life to be arranged to suit him. If he had lived in Geneva under Calvin's rule, he would have found something to amuse him and his readers. 'I have never,' he wrote, 'made an acquaintance that lasted, or a friendship that answered, with any that had not a tincture of the absurd in their character.' It was a generous allowance of this tincture that bound him to Coleridge, whom he revered rightly and laughed at lovingly. It pleased him beyond measure that the poet's mentality should be recognized even when it was least decipherable. During one of Coleridge's early visits to London he put up at a public-house engagingly called 'The Salutation and Cat.' When his money gave out, the landlord, who had sampled his conversation, offered him 'permanent and free entertainment for the good of the house.'

Naturally this delighted Lamb, it was so civilized. It could not happen in England today, and it could never have happened anywhere else. We are patient listeners — we have reason to be — but we are indifferent as to what we hear. Orators, lecturers, speech-makers have dealt heavily with us. We are so accustomed to being talked to that we have well-nigh abandoned the habit of thinking. Dwight Morrow once observed that men did not want to make speeches and did not want to hear them. It was a pure convention. But he said this after dinner, at the unhappy moment when the coffee was being drunk, and the chairman was adjusting his glasses and fumbling with his notes. In his less fretted moods he knew perfectly well that some men do like to talk, and that many men think they like to listen. Why otherwise should they carry radios in their cars to pour out words to them when they might be at peace. Pedestrians, tramping the streets, are startled to hear a volume of sound issuing from a motor, the solitary occupant of which is being instructed concerning politics or tooth-paste. He has reached a depth of mental vacuity which makes the isolation of thought unbearable.

Our good-tempered enjoyment of caricature is an inheritance from England. The modern English caricature retains a likeness, and has an historic value not inferior to that of the cartoon. Indeed the travesty is sometimes so restrained that it resembles an indifferent portrait. The American caricature is content with a single feature, the rest of the face being negligible. Its purpose cannot be mistaken, but the resemblance is often a matter of conjecture. In both England and the States satire and ridicule are made so welcome that they leave behind them only a trail of laughter. The Englishmen who heard themselves mocked at in Gilbert and Sullivan's operas, or in Shaw's more derisive plays, felt, or at least expressed, nothing but pleasure. They were worthy descendants of the Englishmen who nearly two hundred years before had crowded the Lincoln's Inn Theatre to hear themselves degraded in the *Beggar's Opera* to the rank and file of roguery. Something of the same delight was manifested two years ago by Americans who went to see *Of Thee I Sing*, and had explained to them the inglorious nature of their absurdities.

The worst in life, we are told, is compatible with the best in art. So too the worst in life is compatible with the best in humour. Jowett, master of Balliol, said comprehensively that every amusing story must of necessity be unkind, untrue, or immoral; and Plato, putting the worst possible construction on a simple thing, declared that the pleasure of the ludicrous originates in the sight of another's misfortune. This may account for our amused tolerance of crime when we are not its victims. The Master Thief was a humourist whose jests never palled on generations of honest men. His successors today are more daring, more inventive, and occasionally more ironic than he ever thought to be. The thieves who stole the gold cup at Ascot, accomplishing the impossible out of sheer bravado — or shall we say pride in their profession? — the thief who at a bazaar in Lincoln put his stolen purses (emptied) into the pocket of the presiding bishop, were jesters unparalleled. Sir Robert Anderson, who stands responsible for both stories, and whose duty it was to protect officials and prelates from spoliation, could not, as a sportsman, withhold his admiration for such flawlessly humorous transgressions. The Lincoln episode was matched only by Sheridan, who never stole anything, but who, being arrested for drunkenness on the London streets and asked his name, stammered out 'Wilberforce.' The effrontery of laying an unseemly charge against a blameless man is very comical. Perhaps it was attempted more than once by the knights of King Arthur's court.

That the worst in life is compatible with the best in humour was proven conclusively in the four years of the World War. Nothing more lamentable could have befallen mankind, and none who lived through it can forget its daily measure of pain. Yet just as a smug world grew austere under discipline, so a dull world grew diverting to keep itself from heartbreak. It was curious that the neutral nations seemed to have lost the right to joke, and did little but offend; but when the warring nations laughed, their

laughter had in it pride as well as gaiety. This was probably
the case in all great wars, and was in some measure due to
the behaviour and speech of fighting men. Sir Bernard
Pares says that the conversation of soldiers is alike all the
world over. 'The same simplicity, the same sufficient and
direct expression.' Their philosophy is conveyed in the old
tin-panny song:

> 'Tis but in vain
> For soldiers to complain.

They probably do complain, and have complained through
all history, being sure of a sympathetic audience; but the
British Tommy in the World War did not grumble at the
horrors of his life in the trenches, nor at the occasional
blunders for which he paid the cost. These things were part
and parcel of his job. He reserved the vials of his wrath
for the 'strawberry-jam-pinchers'; by which opprobrious
epithet he designated the hard-working and miracle-
performing British Commissariat.

In that fantastic and much read novel, 'The Lost Horizon,'
the hero, Conway, being asked by Father Perrault — aged
three hundred or thereabouts — if he had been unhappy as
a soldier in the World War, replies: 'Not particularly so. I
got mad drunk, and killed and lechered in great style. It was
the self-abuse of all one's emotions, and one came through
it, if one did at all, with a sense of almighty boredom. That's
what made the years afterwards so difficult.'

A very popular note to strike in the year 1934. The author
was, to use Oscar Wilde's neat expression, writing 'at the
top of his voice.' But in 1916 he would have won scant
response, for that winter English eyes were turned lovingly
and laughingly at a good-looking young soldier, Captain

Bruce Bairnsfather of the Royal Warwicks, who in the Christmas issue of the *Bystander* had published a sketch of two badly frightened stragglers caught in a spectacular shower of falling shells. It bore the comprehensive title: 'Well, if ye knows of a better 'ole, go to it.'

There was a jest, a sound and primitive jest, which cave-men had doubtless hurled at one another, and it was given a new depth of feeling. The soldiers were fearfully funny, but their situation was none the less perilous for being comical. England was then in a hole, and knew it. She took that picture and that joke to heart, put them on the stage, made them the background for political cartoons, and squeezed out of them all the gaiety and purpose they could be forced to yield. For the remaining years of the War, Captain Bairnsfather, whether fighting in France or disabled at home, was its most popular annalist. The forty-odd sketches entitled 'Fragments from France' sold by the hundred thousand. His soldiers grew from types to living men. Old Bill, Bert, and Alf, the three friends to whom he dedicated 'Bullets and Billets' because they 'sat with him in the mud,' never failed their public. It was from them that Charlie Chaplin acquired the technique of his camouflage in *Shoulder Arms*. It was from them that trench warfare borrowed its humorous aspects. When their dugout is well under water, Alf remarks apprehensively to Bill: 'They'll be torpedoin' us if we stick 'ere much longer.'

What is the temper of these British Tommies whom Captain Bairnsfather knew so well? Their songs are for the most part sardonic:

> Old soldiers do not die,
> They simply fade away.

They gibe perpetually at one another. Bert looking critically at Alf's photographs and then remarking: 'Well, yer know, I like the one of you in your gas mask best,' is an example of their unsparing wit. They jibe also at that accepted target, the Commissariat, and at the unique discomforts of their habitations. They edge away from horrors as best they can — which was not an easy thing to do. But the dull-witted critics at home who feared lest they should cast ridicule on the British army were a trifle duller than usual. These comic soldiers are fighting men who know the cost of war. The whole heavy propaganda of pacifism has given us nothing in seventeen years to compare with the restrained and compelling tragedy of Bairnsfather's sketch, 'Christmas Day.' No Greek dramatist ever banked his fires more carefully than did this young Englishman. We are shown very little, but we apprehend a great deal. Our taste is unassailed, but our hearts are broken. The sketch called 'Blighty' — two wounded men glimpsing the English coast; the picture of the artist, 'On Leave,' have the same quality, but not in the same degree.

As remarkable in its way as the temper of these drawings is Captain Bairnsfather's account of a Christmas day in Flanders when two little groups of British and German soldiers, their trenches separated by a negligible strip of land, established for themselves an impromptu 'Truce of God.' They stood on their parapets unmolested, they scrambled down and wandered about, inspecting one another curiously and without emotion. They exchanged a few semi-intelligible remarks, a few trifling souvenirs, a little tobacco. Then they slipped back to their respective billets, and to the business of killing. Who can doubt that if the men who fought the World War had been permitted to make the World Peace, they would have infused into it some quality of sense!

Captain Bairnsfather was not the only soldier who found something else to do than kill, and something better to do than drink and lecher. In the winter of 1916 two young Englishmen were sent home on leave. One had been wounded and one had been gassed. One could write verses that were at least lively. One could make sketches that were livelier. Both knew something about wire-pulling at home, and a great deal about simple-hearted fighting in France. They polled their wit and their experience, and produced therewith a little book called 'The Hun Hunters' which was merrily malicious. The malice gave no affront, the merriment could not fail to divert. The men who slipped into soft places were extolled for their discretion; the men who fought in the trenches were given some sound advice — advice that would bear thinking over. If, for example, they mislaid their gas masks, they must be doubly careful to preserve their identity disks.

This jesting with death has always been popular with soldiers. To christen a thrice bombarded scrap of roadway 'Lovers' Walk' was considered a neat witticism. George Birmingham, whose lot lay with the duller, safer, sadder side of the War, bore witness to the part that music played in it, and to the fact that it might have played a greater part had it not been scant and spiritless. Britain economized unwisely on her regimental bands which were supposed to sustain that elusive thing called morale. The favourite songs of the soldiers, as reported in England and in the United States, were sentimental, the favourite airs were easily caught

196

and of a haunting sweetness. But there were others of less renown and of anonymous authorship. They were not sentimental, but ribald, profane, and funny; and they were sung by preference to hymn tunes as being universally familiar. Mr. E. V. Lucas has given us in 'Post-Bag Diversions' the words of an uncensored ditty which seems to have been more exhilarating than it sounds:

> There are Germans over there. Never mind!
> There are Germans over there. Never mind!
>   If they chance to drop a shell,
>   We shall all be blown to Hell,
> There'll be Germans there as well. Never mind!

That the British and, later on, the American soldiers were more jovial than the French was easily accounted for. The enemy was not occupying their territory. There were no 'devastated districts' in their lands. The contrast between the sober fashion in which the French recruits left for the fighting-line and the riotous cheerfulness of the half-trained young Englishmen was very striking. An American official in London who stood watching the crowded station and the departing troops was struck by one old country woman who stood silent and sad by the side of her hilarious son. When she spoke, her voice was low and compelling: 'My boy,' she said, 'I'll miss you.' 'Well, mother,' was the perfectly reasonable reply, 'I hope the Germans will, too.'

If the War, for all its ghastliness, revived the old fighting faith that life is worth the living, that faith found expression in brave jests against an adverse fate. The soldier laughed when he could because he had no reason to suppose he would laugh long. And he was often astonishingly keen. He designated the austere 'Summary of War Intelligence,' issued daily to the British press, as 'Comic Cuts'; not because the material furnished could possibly have amused anybody; but because the cuts eliminated the facts so dextrously as to convey the impression of news when no news was given, the impression of confidence when no confidence was felt. Now and then there is a scholarly flavour to this soldier's wit. The freight cars marked 'Chevaux, 8; Hommes 40' which carried the troops over France had always been a target for mirth; but the British private who quoted with relish Virgil's line, 'Forsitan et illis olim meminisse juvabit,' would have seemed out of place in any other war than this, in which the last limit of astonishment had long since been reached.

Throughout the four years, *Punch* never flinched from its appointed task. Its cartoons were militant, its jests were keen with the almost intolerable keenness of a time when nobody dared to be dull. The matron of the slums who hurled this reproach at a neighbour: 'Call yourself an honest woman with that black eye, and your husband at the front!' gave us first a gasp and then a laugh, which is the order of precedence a good joke should always follow. After the Armistice there was a laudable effort to re-establish sport, and *Punch* portrayed an amiable enthusiast saying to a veteran and very distinguished marksman: 'You'll be glad to have the Bisley Rifle Meeting revived?' To which the marksman replies with languid interest: 'Yes, but there will be some poor scoring. You see there's been no serious shooting for the past four years.' It is impossible to conceive of deeper irony than this. Swift would have shrunk from its implications.

Just as there were hardy souls who defended laughter in

the Middle Ages, sometimes in the spirit of ribaldry, sometimes under the protection of learned writers, so there are unsmiling men and women who today assert that our levity is lacking in intellectual or spiritual value. It is as forced as a hothouse flower and as undistinguished as a weed. The twelfth-century monks knew what they were about when they discouraged the frank merriment which expressed a too keen delight in living. Pious souls like the Shepherd of Hermas had indeed pleaded the cause of gladness: 'For every man that is glad doeth the things that are good and thinketh good thoughts, despising grief.' But such voices were low-pitched compared to the riotous wit which for two hundred years paved the way for Rabelais. Today Rabelais is much in favour. We are advised and entreated to cultivate gaiety in any fashion and at any cost. But when men write semi-scientific papers to encourage their neighbours to laugh, they are pursuing what can never be overtaken. A laugh charms us by its suddenness and unexpectedness, just as an oath impresses us by its suddenness and rarity. The lilt of the unexpected laugh is like the impact of the rare oath. They have everything to gain by infrequency.

Emerson neither laughed nor swore. The humour of Jane Austen made as little appeal to him as did the humour of Dickens or of Cervantes. He had no more need of diversion than he had need of friends or of the world. The comedy of life was played in vain before his attentive eyes. Plato makes Socrates say that men in public life, or holding important positions, should laugh as seldom as possible. He knew how the crowd confuses gravity with wisdom. Lord Chesterfield boasted that nobody had ever heard him laugh, and he adjured his son to abstain from so vulgar an indulgence. 'A man of parts and fashion,' he said, 'is seen to smile, but never heard to laugh.'

Good advice so far as it went. There is no doubt that some superiority attaches itself to people who, like Alice Meynell, are never betrayed into laughter. Socrates could not help attitudinizing, because he was the embodiment of wisdom and virtue in an unworthy age. He stood, of necessity, on a pedestal. Lord Chesterfield was artificial to the core. But we cannot conceive of Emerson as consciously impressive. Whom was there to impress? He had no chance to die for a principle, and no desire to live as a model. He met his fellow creatures with a gentlemanly tolerance that was vastly to his credit; but it was not for their sake that he abstained from laughter.

Mrs. Meynell considered that men and women laugh more frequently and more immoderately than the circumstances of life warrant. They laugh at the wrong time — at serious and even tragic moments in a play, and at sober arguments in a speech — and they laugh fatuously at very foolish jokes. Making every allowance for hilarity that is obviously nervous and artificial, and so does not express merriment at all (Hazlitt thought it did), there is left a superfluity of meaningless laughter that embarrasses intelligent conversation.

This is a fair indictment. Charlotte Brontë would have agreed cordially with Mrs. Meynell. Both these women had, like Dr. Charles William Eliot, a knack of lowering the social temperature. They superimposed more gravity than the occasion called for. Miss Brontë was, so far as we can discover, immaculately free from any taint of humour; but Mrs. Meynell had a keen appreciation of the comic spirit in its best and finest development. Her characterization of Mr. Pecksniff as 'a bright image of heart-easing comedy' is the most perfect tribute ever paid to a creation of Dickens. She felt, as all right-minded readers have felt, bewildered and hurt by the treatment accorded him. The responsibility for meting out rewards and punishments, which lay heavy on the shoulders of Victorian novelists, impelled them to incredible bouleversements in the last Day of Judgment chapters.

'Saints, philosophers, and perfect gentlemen,' so runs the saying, 'may not laugh.' But Saint Theresa laughed heartily. Democritus reached the age of a hundred because he found the follies of mankind more laughable than dispiriting; and many gentlemen, when not balanced on pedestals, have laughed their fill. Nevertheless gravity and a pedestal go a long way. They have shown what they can do in Russia, where the pedestal is high enough for heroics, and the gravity is indigenous. Laughter is a dissipation of energy. The Middle Ages lavished their energy on everything that came along; they had plenty of it to spare. But Russia is conserving hers for a purpose, and cannot afford the waste of merriment, even if she felt disposed to be merry. Were she religiously inclined, her favourite evangelist might have been the Nova Scotian Henry Alline, a man of power and purpose. 'On Wednesday the twelfth,' is a characteristic entry in his journal, 'I preached at a wedding, and had the happiness thereby to be the means of excluding carnal mirth.'

'The wit knows that his place is at the tail of the procession,' said Dr. Oliver Wendell Holmes, who for many years supplied Boston with its daily Atticisms, and who in certain distinguished moments rose high above the level of fun-making. His words have a faintly bitter flavour, but there is always, or almost always, an undertone of bitterness when the jester turns sedate. There is always, or almost always, an undertone of despair when the serious analyze a jest. Nothing, for example, was ever too transparent for Freud to explain painstakingly to his readers. He has been capable of telling them that when a doctor said to the husband of a sick woman, 'I do not like her looks,' he meant he feared the progress of disease; and that when the husband said to the doctor, 'I never did like her looks,' he meant that she had always been uncomely in his eyes. It hurts our pride to have this kindergarten method applied to our adult if languid intelligence. We should like to confront the scientist with Maurois's elusive jest: 'Why should I pay twelve francs for an umbrella when I can buy a bock for six sous?' and see what he would make of it.

Nevertheless there is reassurance in Freud's firm conviction that the pursuit of laughter opens to us certain vistas of delight. Laughter, he says, is a release of static energy, a free and joyous waste of a force which might be stored and utilized. This energy reaches an excessive expenditure in the antics of a clown, and in the uncontrollable mirth they arouse. More agreeably convincing is his certainty that the comic spirit unites intelligent men who are sometimes alienated by other aspects of humour. Wit is a pleasure-giving thing, largely because it eludes reason; but in the apprehension of an absurdity through the working of the comic spirit there is a foundation of reason, and an impetus to human companionship. The beginning of tolerance is mutual understanding, which is difficult to establish without a mutual background. A German analyst of American comic films has confessed his hopeless bewilderment. He says that he has not been brought up to laugh at violence and crime with the artless freedom of Americans. In so far he takes the lead. But there are other points of divergence. Every country has jests of its own, more or less amusing and pleasantly familiar. Now and then one flashes like a meteor across the sky. Now and then one burns its way into the minds of men. When Lamennais observed, '*Les républicains sont fait pour rendre la république impossible,*' he planted a thorn in the human heart, and the wound rankles still.

Happily there are absurdities that soothe as well as witticisms that affront. How far, one wonders, do the householders of other countries share in the American's comic hatred of plumbers? How like are British or French or Swiss plumbers to the lawless men who wreck our happy homes? The oft-repeated tale about the householder who built a bay window, or bought a Ford car, or took a trip to Canada, with some money the plumber did not know he had left, has been foisted upon all American jesters. Charles Dudley Warner probably said it before the day of Ford cars; but Mark Twain usually gets the credit. The joke is only moderately brilliant, but will probably live on until somebody says something as amusing but more unkind to take its place in the heart of a downtrodden public.

It is hard to laugh when one is not amused, and it is hardest when one feels one ought to be amused but knows one isn't. James Payn told us the story of the girl who for years concealed in her breast the guilty knowledge that she did not think 'John Gilpin' funny. As a matter of fact she knew that it was not, and so did most of its readers, and so did Cowper; but it so obviously lacked any other *raison d'être*, and its title, 'The Diverting History of John Gilpin,' carried so plain a challenge, that the poet's long line of admirers agreed to classify it as comedy. They wrote him the kindest of letters to say how heartily they had laughed over the verses which he despised, and they left them to be tucked away in 'Poems for Youth,' or in the department inscribed 'Wit and Humour,' which is a blot upon anthologies.

Yet Cowper did have a lively sense of the ludicrous. It flashes through all his letters until madness overtook him, and it made indiscriminate praise one of the mortifying incidents of life. The worst of a comic sense is that it overrides the vanity which ought to be sweet and consoling. William James, who was not so vain as he had a right to be, tells us of a tragic incident that befell him when he was lecturing at Chautauqua. The wife of a friendly Methodist minister confided to him that she had a newspaper portrait of him on the wall of her bedroom, and underneath it the words, 'I want to bring balm to human lives' — 'supposed,' said the crushed and horror-stricken James, 'to be a quotation from *me!*'

Well, why not? If we don't want to bring balm, we are very much to blame. And if we do want to bring it, we should say so with the convincing candour of politicians and reformers. Our little pots of balm may seem insignificant alongside of their overflowing tanks, but our self-praise may be just as insistent. When Sir Walter Scott went to Ireland he was waited upon at Limerick by an Irish gentleman named O'Kelly, who introduced himself with this highly satisfactory epigram:

> Three poets of three different nations born,
> The United Kingdom in our age adorn:
> Byron of England, Scott of Scotia's blood,
> And Erin's pride, O'Kelly great and good.

204

Scott, who never seemed aware that he had done anything out of the ordinary, was charmed by the breadth of his visitor's views. And, by the same token, he would have sympathized with the abashed William James.

It has been asserted over and over again that the spectacle of pain was enjoyable to the Middle Ages. Nothing could be more untrue. The quality of mercy asserted itself in the beginning of the Christian era; and, throughout all the turmoil that ensued, it shone with a fitful but divine radiance. There were orthodox societies for the promotion of religious persecution which stood in the way of a peaceful life, and were much to be deplored. But historians who point out this discouraging circumstance admit, by way of balance, that there was no really efficacious machinery for protecting the criminal, who had to depend upon his own initiative, and was more than likely to have justice meted out to him. Lawlessness is as old as the first laws it defied or evaded; but never before our age was it so entrenched and protected by legalities. We are no longer liable to be burned at the stake for something which was called heresy, and which theologians alone understood; but we are liable to be robbed with impunity, not only by great and important thieves, but by offenders whose seeming insignificance should be our protection.

As for the spectacle of pain, no one who is not bad beyond redemption can enjoy it; but both men and women can grow hardened to it if it be of necessity a familiar sight. A surgeon in the World War could not afford to retain his sensitiveness to the suffering on every side of him. Children, left to themselves, react unaccountably. A few are moved to pity like the blessed angels in Heaven. Others are hardily indifferent, if not pleased. An adult who falls on the street is the object of concern and commiseration. Children who measure their length with a crash (they fall more lightly than seems possible) are greeted with derisive laughter by their friends. The feeling of pity for the suffering of animals — that wide world of unceasing pain, the knowledge of which is forced by scientists upon our reluctant consideration — is a cultivated sentiment. We may refuse to agree with Mr. Shaw that a cockroach suffering the pangs of unrequited affection is an object pitiful enough to blight the joy of living; but we have learned to recognize emotional qualities in beasts we know, or know about. We see in them the signs and tokens of feelings that are akin to our affections and to our animosities, to our confidences and to our withdrawals. Who can read unmoved the account of the poor chained bear at Southwark Fair, a morose and surly beast which made clumsy overtures of friendship to Dr. Johnson? Of course it did. Years of ill-treatment, years of loneliness and wretchedness and profound distaste for its surroundings had made up that bear's existence. Boys jerked at its chain. Children pelted it from afar. Men passed it with a rough word. Women stared at it unpityingly. Dogs snapped and snarled at a safe distance. Then one day came this strange being, cumbrous and awkward as it was itself; but with everything that spelled intelligence and humanity in its plain features. The bear knew that if it had the possibility of a friend in a friendless world, this was he. It did what it could to show what it had no proper means of showing, and its efforts were comprehensible enough to bring a smile to the faces of those who watched it for a minute before they turned away.

On a par with our sympathy for animals is our sympathy

for those deformities which in a more robust age were considered legitimate subjects for mirth. Comedy, we are given to understand, makes us laugh because it 'breaks the pattern of life'; and what can break the pattern of life more comprehensively than a dwarf? We read in 'Notre-Dame de Paris' that the crowds, the men at least, shouted with laughter whenever they caught sight of Quasimodo. His extreme ugliness filled them with no disgust, it only amused them. In the superb but unsatisfactory film which expressed all the violence of the tale without its depth of emotion, Quasimodo was made so fantastically hideous that no adult would willingly look at him; but the children in the house — who should have been elsewhere — laughed joyously. For them the pattern of life was broken. That was all.

Why did the court of Philip the Fourth desire the dwarfs whom Velasquez painted? It shared this taste with other courts that had no great artist to perpetuate their Gothicisms; but because we are familiar with the unpitying Spanish portraits we marvel most at the solemn King and the restrained Infantas who found amusement in monstrosities. Oscar Wilde, who had a lamentable habit of extracting from a subject the last drop of sentiment it could be forced to yield, told us the story of the 'Infanta's Birthday,' and of the dwarf who died of a broken heart when he discovered how ugly he was. Chesterton used the court dwarfs skilfully, but a bit unfairly, in his description of Philip the Second, a monarch whom it is as easy to disparage as it is difficult to understand:

> King Philip's in his closet with the Fleece about his neck,
> (Don John of Austria is armed upon the deck.)
> The walls are hung with velvet that is black and soft as sin,
> And little dwarfs creep out of it and little dwarfs creep in.

There is no denying that these seemingly harmless lines carry with them an unjustifiable sense of horror. They accord ill with the noble austerity of the Escorial, more like a monastery than a king's dwelling-place, and the only palace in Europe which is a revelation of character. Philip may have had velvet hangings; but all the looms of Genoa would have failed to soften the harshness of his home. As for the dwarfs, they were there to make him laugh, a thing he did so seldom that the occasions which moved him to sudden laughter have become historical. If the dwarfs accomplished this good purpose, they were worth their keep; but as described by Mr. Chesterton they are far from 'bright images of heart-easing comedy.' The pursuit of laughter was no light matter when the Hapsburgs joined the chase.

It has been none too easy since. The era of jesters and fools and dwarfs has long since passed. The distressing era of practical jokes, equally popular in England and on the Continent, survives only as an unhappy memory. It reached its most painful development at the superb court of Louis the Fourteenth (crackers fired under old ladies' chairs and snowballs pelting them in bed); but it lingered fantastically until the days of Marie Antoinette. In England the sport declined when the last Hanoverian king died unlamented. The United States, destitute of kings and courts, lived as humorously as it could on British puns and home-made mis-spelling, both of which have been consigned to oblivion. But the pursuit goes on because of man's craving for diversion. What stage have we reached in a day of comic films and comic strips, clever cartoons and dull jokes, a highly developed school of art which is not meant to be so funny as it looks, and writers galore whom reviewers liken to

Rabelais! They seem to have no other standard of comparison.

When we are contemplating the garnered humour of our world, we may rule out of court the men who are unconsciously humorous. We laugh at them instead of with them, and we give them no credit for diverting us. Cobbett said in all seriousness that 'the gewgaw fetters of rhyme were invented by the monks to enslave the people,' a remark congested with errors. The Calvinistic Synod of Poictiers expressed its conviction that Satan was responsible for the English Liturgy, of which he might have been reasonably proud. Mallet tells us in an access of devout veneration that Voltaire's sensibility was such that he always had a fever on the anniversary of the feast of Saint Bartholomew. It will be observed that these remarks, the fair fruits of pious predilections, belong to the school of absurdities which block the path of civilization. It is probable that Cobbett and the Synod and Mallet did not half believe what they said, but this was no excuse for saying it. 'It is important not to be a fool, but it is very hard,' comments Santayana in one of his more discouraging moments. In view of the fact that none of us can hope to always escape, we cannot but regret the permanence accorded to words which should be instantly forgotten.

The wit and wisdom of humanity is likewise permanent, for which Heaven be praised. The pleasure we derive from a few illuminating words represents one of the alleviations of life, and we owe this pleasure to an understanding of comedy and the comic spirit. The notice posted in the New York stock exchange when Theodore Roosevelt went on his hunting trip to East Africa: 'Wall Street expects every lion to do its duty!' is as good as any historic jest the world has ever known. We cannot imagine a sentiment more tersely or more admirably expressed. It filled the heart of Roosevelt with delight. He could enjoy a joke at his own expense as well as any man in Christendom. This was part and parcel of his robust and enviable courage. When we read that Lady Mary Wortley Montagu exploded with laughter over a caricature of herself, we begin to understand the intrepidity which enabled her to introduce inoculation into England. She had many regrettable qualities, but cowardice and the maladjustments of cowardice were not among them. The labels, 'Not to be shot,' which were hung around the necks of the Trafalgar Square lions when Roosevelt stopped in London on his return from Africa, were certainly funny. They resembled the label, 'Not for sale,' which adorned the Sphinx when Mr. J. Pierpont Morgan visited Cairo. But neither of these excellent jests approaches the stock exchange witticism. They lack its perfection of form and the depth of its laughing malice.

There is a good and growing tendency to terseness in modern wit. The first century to become chary of speech was the eighteenth. It understood the art of elimination. The nineteenth returned in some measure to prolixity because it had so much of importance to say. The twentieth century is patient with expansive seriousness, but curtails its gaiety. People whose object is to amuse must be quick about it. When Samuel Butler, writing in 1664, observed that his countrymen

> Decide all controversies by
> Infallible artillery,

Englishmen were well pleased with his wording, and in comfortable accord with his sentiment. But when, two hundred years later, Walter Bagehot wrote, 'The English argue best in platoons,' we recognized the difference between a thing which is well said and a thing which could not be said better. Augustine Birrell believed that Bagehot was one of the extraordinary men whose remarks are made for the first time. This remark was made for the last time; partly because its form admits of no improvement, and partly because its sentiment is one which has been carefully obliterated from our consciousness. We may no longer plead for the best in art if it expresses an unpopular form of misdoing.

Neatness of phrase is so closely akin to wit that it is often accepted as its substitute. Precepts have come floating down to us — sometimes on the broad stream of history, sometimes in little trickling autobiographies — which survive because they have deftly illuminated a corner of life, preferably of domestic life, to which we have all in our day submitted. 'Vanity should be avoided,' said Saint Louis, whose wisdom kept pace with his sanctity; 'but every man should dress well, in the manner of his rank, so that his wife may the more easily love him.' Since Adam was evicted from Paradise, no better counsel has been given to his successors. By its side we may put these pensive words of Ruskin which illustrate the parental mind: 'My father expected me to write poetry as good as Byron's — only pious; to preach sermons as good as Bossuet's — only Protestant.' The affectionate and tolerant amusement which parents inspire in the minds of their children guarantees peaceful relations. Ruskin sympathized with his father's aspirations. He would have gratified them had it lain in his power. What he did do was just as remarkable. To coerce men into seeing beauty where they did not know, and did not want to know, it existed, was to run single-handed a bloodless revolution.

Humour brings insight and tolerance. Irony brings a deeper and less friendly understanding. No one could accuse Anatole France of friendliness when he wrote, 'The law in its majestic equality forbids both the rich and the poor to sleep under bridges.' A chilling truism which throws all modernity out of gear. But when Elmer Davis observes cheerfully in a morning paper that 'Pedestrians in New York are tolerably safe from everything but traffic,' he is agreeably ironic, and a quick laugh is his reward. Yet poverty and homelessness are minor, because controllable, evils, compared to the loss of life which the American motorist exacts day after day and night after night as the price of his pleasure. Once more we are confronted by our national indifference to bloodshed, provided always it is not spilled voluntarily on the battle-field.

Bernard Shaw is ironical only in his plays; his speech, as recorded, is humorous with a bias toward sentiment. He was manifestly good-natured when he deplored the ill luck of the Venetian fleas which the damp makes rheumatic, and consequently slow, although their existence depends on their activity. He was gentler still when he expressed a desire to be followed to the grave by the animals he had not eaten — a desire which proves he had never seen *Punch's* picture of an old gentleman pursued by an irate bull, and gasping indignantly in his flight: 'And me a vegetarian all my life!' The vision of the grateful beasts following Mr. Shaw's ashes so moved Gilbert Chesterton that he offered himself as an understudy for one of the elephants; a proposition which proves that one jest breeds another, and that all conspire to brighten our sad little planet. *'Après tout c'est un monde passable.'*

Historic witticisms run the best chance of survival. The Stock Exchange joke (too good to be lost) will always find a quiet corner in some discerning narrative, and a grateful chuckle will betray its presence. Beau Brummell's matchless effrontery, 'Who's your fat friend?' must live, because nobody can tell the story of the Prince Regent and leave out Beau Brummell, and nobody can tell the story of Beau Brummell and leave out his last supreme defiance. It is a pleasant thing to remember, because the poor gentleman had grievous treatment at the hands of whilom friends. He was not in the least like Sir Galahad or Sir Philip Sidney; but he was a better man than those who turned from him in his need, and the laugh lies with him.

There are witticisms which do not illustrate any episode in history, but which are inspired by certain changes in our outlook upon life, in our domestic or social relations. We are hardly conscious of what is happening until the difference between yesterday and today becomes suddenly and startlingly manifest. When Augustine Birrell observed in that musing manner which gave him a deceptive air of detachment: 'Now that women have found they can talk about everything, they won't talk about anything else,' he gave perfect expression to a disconcerting truth. It was not a passing phase which attracted the amused Englishman's attention. He understood that the repeal of reticence was permanent. What he failed to grasp was its desirability, and his manner of making this known without saying so is flawless.

The casual remark of a witty Boston woman, Mrs. Bell, that Christian Science was 'good for complaints, but not for

diseases,' sounds French. It has the neat finish of a Gallic
jest, and it was spoken when another change of view was
compelling our attention, when sanguine souls were endeavouring to believe in the triumph of what should be over what
was. The Boston doubter drove her point home. To reach
the core of a subject in a lightly spoken word is an attain-
ment so rare that we can only pay homage to its deftness.

Far below Mr. Birrell's irony and far below Mrs. Bell's
wit is the bewildered but cheerful remark of a nameless
American humourist that he had been told that Wagner's
music was better than it sounds. This also illustrates a period
of transition. Less than a hundred years separate us from
Victorian prudery and the reluctance of well-informed
people to tell all they knew; from the 'malicious magnetism'
of Boston which drove the alarmed Mrs. Eddy to the pure
atmosphere of Concord; from the first performance of *Lohen-
grin* in Dresden. We follow the civilizations of the world by
the jests of the world. Francis Wilson once asked a Philadel-
phia bookseller if he had an expurgated edition of Dr. Watts's
poems. This was typical of the actor, the city, and the day;
but Wilson subsequently admitted that he would never again
venture upon a joke which took so long to be grasped.

We cannot ignore the claim of parody when we are reck-
oning our debt to laughter. The parody is a form of satire,
an effective weapon of ridicule. It has no place by the side
of the original jest which is so rare and so enduring; but it
requires — to be well done — a mixture of verbal dexterity,
of acerbity, and of understanding which is not often forth-
coming. It enjoys an immediate popularity, but is apt to be
short-lived, depending for its existence on the acquaintance

of the public with the work it mocks. One of the best —
if not the very best — of prose parodies is Bret Harte's
'Lothaw.' The parodist did not content himself with string-
ing together the absurdities of the original novel; he reproduced with astonishing fidelity the confiding seriousness
with which Disraeli told his stories to a sophisticated world.
The 'simple but first-class conversation,' with which 'Lothaw'
opens gives us the correct atmosphere. The scene which bids
farewell to Mrs. Camperdown is as good as it is brief. 'How
is she?' asks the youthful hero of the lady's husband whom
he encounters on the street. 'I regret to say that she is dying,'
said the General in a grave voice. 'She wants to see you.
Here is the key of my lodging. I will finish my cigar outside.'

It is perfect in its way; but who in the twentieth century
is going to read 'Lothair' for the sake of laughing at a parody? Who is going to read 'Jane Eyre' (presuming a youth
too recent for her companionship) for the sake of laughing
over 'Miss Mix'? The 'Condensed Novels' are things of the
past, while 'The Luck of Roaring Camp' lives. Mr. Chris-
topher Stone, who wrote a carelessly good little book on
'Parody,' made a bid for its preservation. He admitted that
Calverley set small store by his inimitable 'Fly Leaves,' and
that the 'Rejected Addresses' have been more talked about
than read; but he was sensitive to the homage paid to errant
genius by attentive wit. He recalled to our memories the
shining and somewhat unlovely brilliance of the Yellow
Book. He forbore to rebel at the parodies of Swinburne's
poems, too numerous, and one might say too inevitable, for
enjoyment. He gave the palm of supreme excellence to Mr.
James Stephen's Wordsworthian parody, 'Poetic Lament on
the Insufficiency of Steam Locomotion in the Lake District.'

It is an admirable and malicious imitation of the great poet, but the best thing about it is the title.

Mr. Andrew Lang's parody on 'The Walrus and the Carpenter' is interesting because it shows that one Englishman at least shared the American's abhorrence of plumbers. Mr. Owen Seaman's parody on Mr. Davidson's 'Ballad of the Nun' has the unique merit of using serenely moderate language to express immoderate emotions. Mr. Davidson committed the unpardonable sin of taking a medieval figure, simple, typical, easily understood, winning human sympathy and receiving divine forgiveness, and turning her into an introspective hussy, sinning for sin's sake, and demanding praise for her achievement. Seaman in turn stripped this temerarious young woman of every attribute save bewildered modernity. He described her unkindly as desirous of becoming a 'sex-impressionist,' but not knowing how to set about it:

> Across the sounding City's din
>   She wandered, looking indiscreet,
> And ultimately landed in
>   The neighbourhood of Regent Street.

Surely the words 'looking indiscreet' are a triumph of understatement.

There is one American parody which should survive the desolating years because of its supreme merit and its inspired choice of a subject. Oliver Herford's 'Rubáiyát of a Persian Kitten' has some curious affiliation with such masterpieces as Gray's 'Ode on the Death of a Favourite Cat, Drowned in a Tub of Gold Fishes,' and Prior's amatory verses 'To a Child of Quality.' It is not perfect as they are perfect; but

216

it presents the same quality of adroit and charming precision. Mr. Herford did so much to brighten our dull days that his memory should be held blessed. His eminently well-bred humour was a benefaction while he lived, and should be our inheritance today, were we keen enough to recognize its value. The 'Rubáiyát' is his masterpiece because kittens were the things he loved the best and drew the best (his dogs and cows were of the Noah's Ark variety), and because there is a strong natural likeness between a Persian kitten and a Persian philosopher. The thoughts and the speech of one are singularly fitted to be the thoughts and the speech of the other. The kitten surveys the world tolerantly, attentively, drawing correct conclusions, and wise with the wisdom of the spectator. He is too young for amorous adventures under the compelling moon, and with single-hearted devotion follows the dictates of his greed. But being a philosopher as well as a little cat, he casts over the object of his desires (the fish in the ice-box for example) a network of pleasant fancies that would do credit to his prototype:

> What if the Sole could fling the Ice aside,
> And with me to some Area's haven glide —
>   Were't not a Shame, were't not a Shame for it
> In this Cold Prison crippled to abide?

> Some for the Glories of the Sole, and Some
> Mew for the proper Bowl of Milk to come.
>   Ah, take the fish and let your Credit go,
> And plead the rumble of an empty Tum.

Dr. Horace Howard Furness always insisted that the last four lines were the most perfect parody in the English language. Competitions are soul-destroying, but they are certainly very good.

Steele thought it the part of humanity to laugh at a poor joke. He was a kind-hearted man who doubtless encouraged bores, forgetting that the poor joke is far from being despised or rejected. Its appeal is as wide as is the stupidity of the world, and we know its tenacity by the number of times we listen to it. As a matter of fact, nothing is harder than for the brilliant and concentrated mind to grasp the magnificent implications of popularity. Hazlitt, who had moments of illumination, confessed in one of them that he had been pardonably impatient over the endless pages which describe Miss Harriet Byron's wedding-clothes, until he found that two young ladies had faithfully copied these pages for their private and particular delight. That taught him a lesson. Richardson's appeal was universal. Cooks in English kitchens read 'Pamela' (we have Augustine Birrell's word for it), spinsters in English drawing-rooms read 'Sir Charles Grandison,' and all England and France wept copiously over 'Clarissa Harlowe.'

If a poor joke is hard to kill, a good joke lives long, sometimes in retirement, sometimes flashing its cheerful light across our path, and helping us to go merrily to Heaven. We are occasionally asked to believe that the infirmities of the spirit are chastened by laughter and purified by pain. They are neither. Infirmities of the spirit accompany us through life, held in check only by the astringency of discipline. The cheerful philosophers who set at naught the funded experience of mankind mislead their followers. We are a little like the Scotch brownie, Wag-at-the-Wa, whose perpetual toothache failed to extinguish his perpetual mirth. Therefore the laugh that is not the laugh of senility raises our spirits, and the 'finely tempered smile,' so honoured by Mr. Meredith, restores our balance and control. Good little stories — the kind that are strewn about the pathways of eminent men — are as beneficial as the best of jests. There is one told of Arthur Balfour, who was held up at Dumfries in the third year of the World War. A Scotland Yard official begged him to avoid recognition, and the statesman replied he was sorry, but he had already signed his name in the lift-boy's birthday book. As an illustration of England's fundamental democracy, this anecdote is pleasant and humorous. President Coolidge's musing remark, 'I see the statue of Washington still stands,' has the same quality of tranquil reassurance.

On the preservation of the Comic Spirit depends in some measure the ultimate triumph of civilization. Science may carry us to Mars, but it will leave the earth peopled as ever by the inept. Wealth will be a bone of contention as long as men stay men. Laughter, which was ineffectively suppressed in the Middle Ages, will be ineffectively pursued in ages of intensive enlightenment. The bitter humour of the political cartoonist keeps it alive, but there is an acrid quality in his mirth. It stings, but it does not heal. Mr. Meredith, contemplating the situation at the close of the nineteenth century, reached two conclusions with which the twentieth century reluctantly agrees. First, that we should never again laugh the careless laugh of the Middle Ages when the sea of human delight rose perilously high; and second, that the Comic Spirit is not sufficiently diffused to be a safeguard. Nation by nation he scrutinized, and nation by nation he found wanting:

'The Germans are kings in music, princes in poetry, good speculators in philosophy, and our leaders in scholarship. But the discipline of the Comic Spirit is needful to their growth.'

'The English excel in satire, and are noble humorists. The Comic Spirit is different; but they have the basis for this spirit in their esteem for common sense. They cordially dislike the reverse of it. And they are given to looking in the glass. They must see when something ails them.'

The French? Well it is their inspiriting task to fire the faggots piled by the industry of the world. Their passion for logical issues, for reason, for orderly mental processes is too keen to permit of mirth. Whatever they may have been in the Middle Ages, they are not now a laughing nation. They seem by tradition, temper, and schooling eminently fitted to grasp the Comic Spirit; yet they have permitted more than one giant absurdity to block their path to progress.

Of Russia we know very little. She was sad at heart in the old days, from the Tzar on his throne to the peasant at his plough, and this sadness was reflected in her art and letters. Grave and serious today, she presents a blank surface to our consideration. We have bitter books written by suffering exiles. We have sanguine books written by propagandists, and heavy with documents. But none of them tell us what Russia is really like; what her toiling millions are eating and drinking (a matter of supreme importance); how her middle classes (no middle class ever gets permanently wiped out) are conducting the traffic by which they live. From a censored press we learn little. From personally conducted tourists we learn nothing at all, save that Moscow is probably the most overpopulated city in the world. Only now and then a Russian joke comes wandering over the earth, and Russia seems alive again. It is almost always a joke at the expense of the Soviet, and this is a cheering circumstance. If a sternly repressive government can awaken (and let us trust tolerate) an adverse jest, there is hope for humanity yet.

The mirth of America was of a simple texture. The Puritan felt no need of a Comic Spirit; the Quaker would not have known what to do with it; the cotton-grower of the South could never have been persuaded that he lacked it; the pioneer who trekked into the wilderness made up his own rough and ready fun as he went along. We have outgrown several layers of civilization, we have outlived repeated degradations of public service. It is not hard for us to recognize absurdities; but we are content with recognition. We cannot be made to understand their danger. Our passionate loyalty to our humourists, our tolerance of the 'comics' in newspapers and cinemas, proves our need of laughter; but we are not gay. The appalling grin with which men and women are photographed for the press is as remote from gaiety as from reason.

The learned Hallam stretched the Dark Ages to the very verge of the fifteenth century. Not until 1495 did he see any reason to consider men even imperfectly educated. It is true that in 1438 one Laurenzes John Koster of Haarlem, a painstaking and scholarly man, printed with blocks a book of 'images and letters.' Its leaves were loose, and pasted together when complete; and it was devoutly entitled *Speculum Humanæ Salvationis*. Twelve years later, John Gutenberg cut his metal types, the Mazarin Bible was printed, and book-learning was on its way to revolutionize the world. A great and glorious event, immensely satisfactory to Hallam and to the rest of us. But in 1091, before the first Crusade swept Europe, the foundations of the southern spire of Chartres Cathedral were securely laid; and in 1145 the West Portal was standing as it stands today, its mutilated statues surviving the wreckage of centuries. The Church Militant, the Church Triumphant, the love of men for Christ, the pity of Christ and of his holy Mother for men, the beauty of holiness, the dignity of history (so Henry Adams points out), all find expression in this portal. It has 'the grand air of the twelfth century, as indestructible as the grand air of a Greek temple.' Three hundred years before Laurenzes John Koster fitted together the pages of his first book, medieval France gave to her unlettered, beauty-loving sons this noble education.

Nearly four hundred years ago the great Elizabeth ascended the throne, and 'merry England' began in sober earnest the pursuit of lost laughter. Two hundred and fifty years ago the 'merry monarch,' who had pursued it so hard and so unavailingly, closed his tired eyes in death. The eighteenth century, which came nearer than any other to the Comic Spirit and the 'finely tempered smile,' went its way; and the boisterous high spirits of the early nineteenth century drooped and were lost in measureless confusion before it closed. Today we make scant pretence of cheerfulness; and absurdities, when recognized, seem insurmountable to some and inspirational to others. Strange coercive drives pursue us relentlessly, and leave us drained of purpose. And ever and always the ill-organized pursuit goes on:

> I cry a reward for a Yesterday,
> Now lost, or stolen, or gone astray,
> With all the laughter of Yesterday.

INDEX

INDEX

229

EASTERN DISTRICT HIGH
227 Marcy Avenue—Brooklyn, N. Y.

INDEX